Ten principles for husb

The Marriage Commandments

John Diffenderfer

The Marriage Commandments
Copyright © 2015 by John Diffenderfer. All rights reserved.

No part of this publication may be used, transmitted, copied, or reproduced without written permission of the author or publisher except in brief quotations.

Quantity discounts are available on bulk purchases of this book for resale, educational, fundraising, or event purposes. For more information, visit, www.TheMarriageCommandments.com.

ISBN: 978-0-692-45765-8

Printed in the United States of America.

Disclaimer:
While the author has used his best efforts in preparing this book, he make no representations with respect to the accuracy of the contents of this book and specifically disclaims any implied guarantees or fitness for a particular purpose. The advice and strategies contained herein may not be suitable for your situation. You should consult a professional where appropriate. The author shall not be liable for any loss or damages.

Throughout this book, names and identifying details (excluding Biblical references) have been changed to protect the privacy of individuals. Any seemingly direct identification of actual persons, living or dead, is purely coincidental.

To my wife.

Contents

Introduction   1

Zero   5
I am the Lord, thy God.

One   17
You shall have no other gods before me.

Two   27
Thou shalt not make unto thee any graven image.

Three   37
Thou shalt not take the name of the Lord, thy God, in vain.

Four   49
Remember the Sabbath day to keep it holy.

Five   57
Honor thy father and thy mother.

Six   **67**
Thou shalt not kill.

Seven   **79**
Thou shalt not commit adultery.

Eight   **87**
Thou shalt not steal.

Nine   **95**
Thou shalt not bear false witness against thy neighbor.

Ten   **105**
Thou shalt not covet.

The Marriage Commandments

Introduction

This book is unlike most of the marriage self-help books that fly off booksellers' shelves. And there are a lot of those. Doing a quick search for "marriage" among Amazon's book inventory produces well more than one hundred thousand results. Those books often try to reduce marriage to simple, one-size-fits-all formulas. ("If you do this and that, your marriage will improve!") Their prescriptions are finite and dosed out in tasty syrups. Generally, they make their readers feel good and they may treat a few symptoms, but they rarely seem to have lasting effects. Every day, divorce courts and lawyers' offices are filled with folks who have collectively spent countless dollars buying books to try to improve their failing marriages. Comparing the number of books sold to modern divorce rates, one could argue that marriage self-help books are the snake oil of the twenty-first century.

The mistake often made in the pages of the best-selling marriage books is the attempt to reduce the infinite complexity of life down to a finite set of factors. Such books take their factors of choice and focus solely on the management of those particular matters. For instance, one author may feel that selflessness is the lone key to a happy marriage. Meanwhile, a rabbi may publish a book stating that sexuality is the foremost important marital factor. Another author may write a book that focuses solely on the importance of understanding husbands' and wives' unique, gender-specific desires and needs. All of that advice is probably good, but it's limited. Basing a marriage on sexuality, for instance, is only beneficial if both parties are sexually functional. Such factor-centric advice is finite. As such, it can't be a sufficient foundation upon which someone can build something as infinitely complex as a healthy marriage. The universe itself teaches that an infinite creation requires an infinite source.

Fortunately, God is infinite, and God put His infinite nature and wisdom into the truths contained in the Bible. From there, one can discover an everlasting foundation for marriage.

This book tries to avoid building a foundation on finite things. Instead of focusing on a handful of factors and providing lists of tactical, how-to instructions, this book focuses on dynamics that affect every aspect of humanity's infinite lives. The ideas put forth in this book will require you to be diligent. You will have to arrive at your own conclusions. You will need to decide how to apply the principles to your own life and marriage. While the principles are universal, their application should never be reduced to one-size-fits-all "solutions." The everyday choices that stem from these principles may heal your marriage, but those same choices might be toxic to someone else's. The day-to-day tactics that work for one couple may not be effective for another, but the overarching truths and perspective drawn from God's commandments are universal. Marriages are as complex and varied as the individuals who comprise them. As such, this book requires critical thinking, intelligence, and introspection. This is not rocket science — it's infinitely more complex.

This book is designed to provide a framework for the improvement of marriages. As such, the recommendations and principles presented in this book are given with the assumption that one is in a marriage worth maintaining. However, not all marriages merit preservation. Biblically and ethically, divorce can be the best path forward for those with marriages that are either dangerous or compromised through adultery. A person who has an abusive, dangerous, or unfaithful spouse should immediately seek safe, professional advice. This book is not intended for people facing such marriages. The concepts presented in this book are not universally applicable for those with such fundamentally flawed marriages. In some cases, divorce is the proper resolution.

Beyond the baseline premise that your marriage is one worth improving, the ideas presented in this book hinge on four additional presumptions:

1. **You and your spouse are both believers in Christ.**

   If you are not believers, the advice in this book will not be interpreted as intended. As such, it will not be implemented as intended. Thus, the results will likely differ from what was intended. Furthermore, the best marriages are comprised of men and women who share the same spiritual understanding. If you and your spouse are on different pages theologically, it will be difficult for you to successfully adopt a theologically-based perspective for your marriage.

2. **You and your spouse are both sane.**

   If you are not generally sane, working through a logical approach to marriage will be difficult. Mental illness is real, and it is impossible to rationalize with the irrational. Granted, even a broken clock is right twice a day.

3. **You and your spouse both understand that the success and quality of your marriage is one hundred percent each of your individual responsibilities.**

If you are not wholly committed as an individual to improve your marriage, this will likely prove to be an exercise in futility. Great marriages only happen when both the husband and the wife believe that they are each, fully and independently, responsible for the success and quality of their marriage. Don't waste time and energy trying to share the responsibility or place the blame. It's your marriage. Own it.

4. **You and your spouse both want to remain married to one another forever.**

This should be a bit of a no-brainer. However, for many married couples, this is not the case. If you are looking for a way out of your marriage, or if you are looking for excuses to fault your spouse, read no further. This book shouldn't be used as a measuring stick for the evaluation of the shortcomings of your spouse.

If any of these presumptions do not accurately describe you and your spouse, this may not be the book for you. You are, of course, encouraged to read this book and learn as much as you can, but the end result will likely be less than what was hoped for. Fortunately, the world is filled with books on the topic of marriage. Perhaps one of those other books would better suit your worldview or situation. However, if these presumptions fit, please read on. And thank you for making it past the introduction.

Chapter Zero
I am the Lord, thy God.

At the foot of a mountain, an army of slaves waits.

They had left the only home they had ever known. Everything was uprooted. For four hundred years, they had been part of the most powerful society in the world. The only homes they had ever known were behind them, over the dunes, beyond the sea, beside the pyramids. They had left Egypt.

Now, this hoard of peasants is waiting. Anxious. Uncertain. Uncomfortable.

At the start of most weddings, brides and grooms generally feel like the ancient Israelites, unsure and uneasy. This angst doesn't come just from stage fright, nor is it tied just to the magnitude of what is about to take place, though those certainly don't help to still quaking hearts. The feeling is much deeper. It reaches to the core of a person. What brides and grooms often face is a profound shift in identity. Their lives are being redefined and relabeled. Along with this realignment comes an enormous set of expectations, imposed by both self and society. For the bride and the groom, regardless of whether the sum of their emotions is joy or terror, it's unsettling. And it often doesn't resolve by the time the rice is in the air.

They've left Egypt. They're standing before a mountain. Everything that they have known and experienced about their lives is in the process of being transformed.

At Mount Sinai, God gave the Israelites the Ten Commandments. This list of instructions was essentially God's marriage contract with the Israelites. It outlined the terms and conditions of the relationship and listed what actions could essentially invalidate the contract. If the Israelites wanted to remain in a loving, healthy relationship with God, they had to abide by the terms of the Ten Commandments. However, as in most legal agreements, there were consequences for breaking the contract. If the Israelites chose to go against the terms of their covenant, they would sacrifice their relationship with God.

From that ancient culture to this day, Jewish brides and grooms sign marriage contracts as part of their nuptial arrangements. These documents, known as *ketubot* (or a *ketubah*, singularly), are essentially marriage contracts. They contain the marriage vows and outline a list of goods and services that will be provided by each party to the other. Traditional ketubot aren't particularly romantic or sexy. The traditional Jewish text is bluntly written, as one might expect from the pen of an ancient Jewish lawyer. What they may lack in prose, ketubot make up for in clarity. They're very precise, describing in detail exact actions that will be taken by the bride and the groom to secure the marriage. Ketubot outline the legal terms of marriages and serve as binding documents in Jewish ceremonial law. Since the first century, signing a ketubah has continued to be a critical part of what makes a Jewish marriage a marriage.

Likewise, God provided the Israelites with a ketubah. (The very first ketubah, actually.) He wrote His on slabs of stone. In doing so, God clearly outlined the boundaries of His marriage to humanity.

In the book of Ephesians, the Apostle Paul provides marriage advice. He tells husbands to love their wives, just as Christ loved the Church. This is a strong statement. Paul says the Church is the bride of Christ and that husbands should treat their brides the same way God treats His.

Spouses should treat one another as God treats His spouse. The arena in which spouses interact with one another is marriage. As such, human marriages ought to mirror His marriage. Just as Christ's love for His bride should be emulated, God's marriage is also a template for how all marriages should be.

As you will read in this book, the Ten Commandments, God's marriage contract with His bride, provide the parameters within which marriages can flourish. Like a ketubah, the Ten Commandments are the stark boundaries. Within those boundaries, there are a lot of details that fill in the marriage and add complexity, nuance, and value. While the resulting actions may vary depending circumstances, the foundational tenets behind each of the Ten Commandments hold universal truths.

Certainly, the Ten Commandments outline humanity's marriage to God. They also, however, provide a template within which husbands and wives can structure their own marriages. By following God's example — by loving one's spouse the way God loves His — one is able to experience a truly divine marriage. The Ten Commandments outline God's marriage. As such, by definition, they also outline what it means to truly have a Godly marriage.

In the wilderness, God married His people. Reaching down from Heaven, God carved His marriage contract into stone and gave it to His bride, the Israelites. In this contract were ten vows. If the Israelites kept the vows, their marriage and their lives would flourish. If they violated the vows, they would find themselves separated or even divorced from God.

To begin this covenant, God stated simply:

"I am Yahweh, your God, who brought you out of the land of Egypt."

This statement isn't just the wedding stationery. In this simple phrase, God is providing His bride with a clear sense of identity. He is stating who He is and what His role is in her life. He is Yahweh. He is the Israelite's God. The One to whom gratitude was owed for their deliverance from Egypt.

The Israelites desperately needed a sense of identity. Their background was Egyptian. They were accustomed to living in a culture that embraced many gods. The gods of the Egyptians were a buffet, you could choose which one was "yours" and there was no need for exclusivity. Egyptian religion was promiscuous — both literally and figuratively.

In the time leading up to their marriage at Mount Sinai, the Israelites obviously knew about Yahweh. What they didn't yet know was what their relationship with Yahweh would be. Obviously, Yahweh was *a* god. What hadn't yet been stated was that Yahweh would be *their* God. The clarity of Yahweh's claim over them was profound. Their identity within the relationship was definite. The roles were clearly defined. And, through understanding the identity of their God, the Israelites were expected to be inherently grateful, as they quite literally owed their lives to Him.

A clear sense of identity is essential for a healthy marriage. It's very simple but often overlooked. Without a stark definition of the roles within a marriage, there can never be a healthy sense of identity and it is impossible to fully understand the true sense of gratitude that should be inherent in the relationship.

You are husband and wife.

They are yours.

You are theirs.

Husband and wife.

Newlyweds often struggle with a profound lack of security in their relationships, because they fail to acknowledge that their identities have changed. The other person is no longer just their fiancé. They are no longer part of their parents' households. Their friends have all just been demoted in priority, by virtue of the promotion of their new spouse. Everything is upended. And some couples — including many with decades-long marriages — never make it through this identity crisis.

Failure to clearly acknowledge who you are will always lead to conflict.

Once married, you are no longer merely friends, partners, buddies, fiancés, boyfriend or girlfriend, or anything else. You are also not your spouse's judge, parent, police officer, task master, slave, student, or subordinate. You are something much more romantic, more intimate, more committed, and more compassionate. You are a husband or a wife.

You must acknowledge, to each other and to yourselves, who you are and who your significant other is. You are no longer just what you were. You are married. You are now more.

Ashley married Kevin. This happy event followed two years cohabitation. That is to say they had been "shacking up," "playing house," and "living in sin." Shortly after their marriage, they were miserable. They were uncomfortable with each other and uneasy about the future of their relationship.

Their problems were manifest in a wide array of petty conflicts. Their accusations were typical. Ashley spent too much time with her friends. Kevin spent too much money at bars on the weekends. Both were routinely annoyed with one another.

They held separate bank accounts. They made career choices autonomously. Their social circles were largely disparate. When they spent time together, it was only the result of happenstance and boredom — not intention.

Their problem wasn't simply that they had shared a home prior to their nuptials, though that certainly didn't help the matter. Their problem was that they didn't fully identify as being a husband and a wife. They didn't understand the gravity of their new relationship.

Ashley and Kevin still identified foremost as roommates.

Though married, their commitments to each other were minimal. They didn't see any value in making sacrifices for one another's benefit. They didn't strive to sync the pace of the lives or align their ambitions. The respect that they demonstrated toward each other was casual; it was no more than what a friend would show toward another friend. They made jokes at each other's expense. The virtue of courtesy wasn't on their radars. Throughout the course of the marriage, they were never considerate enough to seriously and proactively discuss decisions that would affect both of them. They took their relationship lightly.

They never identified as being a husband and a wife. They lacked that most-important aspect of true self-awareness.

Eventually, they divorced.

CHAPTER ZERO

So what should be the identity of a husband and a wife? Many answers to this question are obvious: united partners, a support system, helpers, guides, lovers, and so forth. Most people understand these basic ideas. Yet, anywhere from about a third to a half (depending on whose data you read) of all marriages fail. So, perhaps there is something missing from the garden-variety descriptions of the roles of marriage.

In Genesis 2, God noticed that Adam was lonely.

"It's not good for a man to be alone," Yahweh surmised. "I will make a helper that is suitable for him."

So, God made Eve, the first spouse.

Eve's role, first and foremost, was to be Adam's "helper." Most English translations of this verse say that this helper, Eve, was supposed to be "suitable" or "right for" Adam. However, the original Hebrew Bible has somewhat of a different take on this word. Instead of "right for," the original writers of the Bible used a variation on the Hebrew word "*neged*." Neged literally means "in front of," "directly facing," and "opposite to." Essentially, God made Eve, the first spouse, to be Adam's "directly opposite" helper. She was intended to help Adam by being in front of him, as his direct opposite.

Eve was made to be Adam's reflection.

Eve's role was to mirror Adam.

Consequently, as with any mirror, what Adam saw in Eve was only his own reflection. Through Eve, Adam was able to see who he really was. Eve's identity was a reflection of Adam, and Adam's identity could only be discovered through Eve. The elements of Adam's character received their value through Eve's reflection. For instance, Adam could only know whether or not he was kind based on Eve's reflection of his behavior.

So what is the identity of a husband and wife? Like Adam and Eve, they are to be mirrors of each other. Just as a clear lake reflects whatever stands before it, so too do husbands and wives reflect one another. Husbands and wives reflect each other's character, behavior, and spirits. Truly self-aware spouses understand that their identity is intrinsically tied to the life of their spouse. They view themselves as extensions (or reflections) of their spouses.

The Bible teaches that God has planned believers' lives. For that matter, He also planned their marriages. Your spouse did not become your spouse by accident, even if you had no idea what you were getting into back when you signed your wedding certificate. God has brought you together to serve each other. God selected your mirror precisely because it is able to perfectly reflect you.

In Spain, it is commonly said that one's spouse is *"Mi media naranja."* Literally, this means "My orange half." The idea behind this citric term of endearment is that when an orange is cut in two, each half perfectly fits and aligns to the other half. Essentially, at the cut, the orange halves are mirror images of each other. Instead of having a "better half," this saying promotes the idea that each side is an equal, perfect match: a mirror.

The thing about mirrors is that they tell the truth. If you don't like what you see in a mirror, you don't try to change the mirror. Instead, you change yourself or your environment. In doing so, you change the image in the mirror.

Great marriages do not come from one party trying to change the other. If you try to change your spouse, you will only smudge or crack your mirror. The mirror is simply a reflection of you. To change what you see in your mirror, you must change yourself. And, quite obviously, you are the only person that you can change.

If asked and promised confidentiality, most spouses could produce long lists of defects that they perceive in their respective significant others. For instance, he or she is lazy, disinterested, impulsive, insecure, overweight, unresponsive, immature, unaccountable, dishonest, arrogant, overbearing, a workaholic, and so on. They focus on the defects of their mirror, instead of realizing that the defects are likely their own — or at least they are the result of their own influence on their spouse.

Furthermore, since God planned your life and your marriage, perhaps the very thing that most bothers you about your spouse is the very thing that God is trying to draw your attention to in your own life. But, why stop there? Let's take it a step further. What if *every single thing* that bothers you about your spouse actually stems from a flaw that resides inside of you?

Everything.

Think about it. When you're honest with yourself, you will be able to connect the dots between your spouse's "flaws" and your own. Every time.

That is not to say that people are not to blame for their own mistakes. Certainly, sane people have the ability to govern their behavior, and they should be expected to do so in a positive, healthy manner. That, however, doesn't remove the link between you and your spouse. You have an impact on your spouse's life. You influence their behavior. Furthermore, aside from what your spouse may or may not do, your perception of your spouse is your own perception. If you are bothered by what you perceive within your spouse, you should recognize that your irritated state is a reaction produced by your mind. Whether or not your spouse's behavior is justified, you should first evaluate your reaction against your own self. Your spouse is accountable for his or her behavior. You, however, are accountable for your reaction.

What if your negative perceptions of your spouse are actually the result of defects in your own life? Imagine a marriage wherein a husband is perpetually agitated by his wife's impulsivity (for some, this won't be difficult). What if the true source of his frustration is actually just his own insecurities, which drive him to crave control and foreknowledge of every aspect of their lives? If one person is impulsive and the other is a control freak, who really needs to change? Who is right? They're both reflections of each other. Her impulsivity feeds his sense of insecurity. Likewise, his controlling nature motivates her to seek moments of abandon. But harmony is possible.

Regardless of who takes the first step, the other will follow. For instance, if the husband learns to let go of his insecurities, he will be less annoyed by his wife's spontaneity. In turn, as he releases his controlling grip, she may feel less of a "need" to "let it go" and do impulsive things. And slowly, their reflections will move closer together.

Paul is a depressed man. His depression is no doubt made worse by the consequences of his poor life choices. Paul's marriage is terrible. Everyone who knows Paul knows that.

One day, Paul confided in some friends that he didn't find his wife attractive. At all. Under any lighting.

Paul blamed his wife's homely appearance for his ongoing addiction to porn. He reasoned that his libido needed an outlet but his wife's unkempt appearance removed her from the list of possible outlets. So porn was his "only option." Paul claimed that because his wife was unattractive, he had to resort to porn.

In truth, because of Paul's misdirected lusts, he no longer thought his wife was attractive. The more porn he consumed, the less attractive he felt his wife was. Subconsciously, he compared his wife to the people on his computer screen. By continually — *ahem* — exposing himself to ever-increasingly unrealistic portrayals of beauty and sexuality, he was unintentionally raising the bar with regard to what he found exciting.

To a simple mind, it's a "chicken or egg" conundrum. Only Paul got it wrong. The results proved that. Instead of realizing that the porn caused him to feel that his wife was unattractive, he instead felt that his "unattractive" wife caused him to spend time watching porn. To this day, he is miserable and his marriage is in shambles.

Instead of seeing a flaw in his mirror and recognizing it as a defect in his own character, Paul instead blamed his mirror. Paul should have rightly identified his waning affections for his wife as a warning sign of his online indiscretions. But he didn't. When his perception of his reflection changed, he failed to rightly attribute it to the changes in his own life.

Kim was always upset with her husband, Jake. Among other complaints, she hated that he was always unwilling to talk about his emotions. Granted, Jake never talked about his emotions.

After nearly two decades of marriage, Kim used this flaw as the excuse to end her marriage.

Kim blamed her mirror.

Instead of blaming Jake for not being more forthcoming about his emotions, Kim should have examined the reflection of her mirror and used it to better align her own life. Rather than blaming her mirror, Kim should have turned her critique inward.

In truth, Kim over-shared and over-indulged her emotions. She was always hyper-dramatic about everything. On a daily basis, she had some new scandal to tell about her co-workers, the cashier at the bakery, her children' teachers, or whomever had popped up on her radar that day.

If she had mounted the courage to look inward, she might have recognized that Jake was serving to temper her unhealthy emotions and gossip. He was subconsciously reflecting and overcompensating for her. The problem is that by being excessively reserved, Jake unknowingly highlighted his wife's soap opera tendencies.

Had Kim exercised sufficient self-control, Jake just might have felt secure enough to share his feelings with her. As it were though, she was a wrecking ball, and he hid. And the more he hid, the more she destroyed.

For a marriage to thrive, both parties must fully understand and embrace their identities and roles. You are not merely friends. (Nor are you enemies.) Ultimately, you are either her husband or his wife. An extension and a reflection of one another. Nothing less.

It is not your job to fix your spouse. You are not their parent. You cannot fix your spouse. You are not God. As a husband and a wife, you are mirrors of one another. You have the spouse you deserve. Your spouse exists to help you identify the flaws in your own life. In that way, above all else, your spouse is your other half. That is your identity.

Chapter One
You shall have no other gods before me.

The first of the Ten Commandments is simple; it was God's demand for exclusivity. The Israelites were His bride, and nothing was to get between them. God was essentially saying that, for their marriage to work, the Israelites had to curb their inclinations toward others. He did not want an open marriage.

God wasn't interested in being part of a pantheon. This was a bold demand. The Israelites had just spent four centuries deeply entrenched in Egypt's pantheistic society. (To put that in perspective, that's more time than the entire history of the United States.) Pantheism was the norm for every other person that they had ever met, and it had been that way for many, many generations. It ran so deep, that even when God talked to Moses through the burning bush, Moses didn't recognize Him or know His name. What's more, in that encounter, Moses even referred to Yahweh as the "God of your [the Israelites'] fathers." In that simple statement, Moses failed to identify himself as being an Israelite and he described Yahweh as being someone else's God — as opposed to *his* God. Naturally, having been raised in Egypt, Moses may have been ignorant of many things, including monotheism.

Against that backdrop, Yahweh demanded exclusivity. Certainly, this commandment has direct ties to marital fidelity. A healthy marriage can't exist without exclusivity. It was true of God's marriage to Israel, and it's true of your marriage.

Fundamentally, a marriage is an agreement of mutual exclusivity. As husband and wife, you have agreed to share a heightened level of intimacy and commitment with one another and to not share it with anyone else. When you let others into your marriage, you give away some of the very thing that makes marriage, marriage. You have to guard your marriage from everyone and everything else.

This exclusivity goes far beyond just sexual relations. Many people mistakenly feel that they have exclusivity in their marriages simply because they don't have sex with anyone other than their spouse. That's a degree of exclusivity, but it's not comprehensive exclusivity. In this commandment, God didn't limit the exclusivity of His marriage to any individual aspect of His relationship with Israel (such as prayer, worship, or obedience, for example). God wanted exclusivity in all aspects of His relationship. Likewise, you should also be equally liberal in your exclusivity. Your spouse must absolutely have exclusive access to you, on every level. If your marriage isn't exclusive, it's going to be rough.

Several years had passed since Mary had seen Katherine, a childhood friend. In that time, Katherine had married and divorced her high school sweetheart. Like most recent divorcées, her attitude about the situation was one of self-righteous indignation and feigned bewilderment about how this seemingly "out of the blue" marital disaster had occurred.

CHAPTER ONE

"Mark just couldn't understand that Phillip was my best friend. I mean, I couldn't just stop being friends with my best friend just because I was married," said Katherine.

But Mark was her husband.

Was.

Phillip was gay. The friendship he shared with Katherine was strictly platonic. Nevertheless, even though they never shared even a hint of sexual interest in one another, their relationship was infidelity. Together, they crossed boundaries of the heart and mind. Philip and Katherine had an emotional connection that was greater than Katherine's emotional connection to her husband, Mark.

Katherine had let Phillip in. Instead of having an exclusive relationship with her husband, Katherine considered Phillip to be her foremost confidant and counselor. She admitted this openly and with a degree of pride. She thought that she had a sitcom life: a husband for sex and security and a gay best friend for lifelong companionship. She thought it was fabulous; she had collected the perfect cast of friends to play on the set of her life.

The only problem was that real life never fit in the alternate reality of a television show. Real life has consequences. Real people have feelings and insecurities that are made worse by the self-indulgent behavior of others. People get hurt. Real marriages have to be exclusive.

Exclusivity can be accomplished in two ways. One is positive. The other is not.

From the human perspective, nearly everything is viewed in shades of relativity. A Honda Accord is a relatively fast car, especially when compared to a Ford Pinto. However, when the Pinto is gone and the only other cars on the road are Aston Martin V12s, the Accord suddenly seems a little sluggish.

In the same way, views of marital exclusivity are subjective and relative. You may feel that your spouse has exclusive access to your emotions, because they are the only one to whom you have revealed your deepest hopes and fears. But, is that exclusivity because you have given them more access or because you have restricted access from everyone else? Is your marriage exclusive because you have elevated your intimacy with your spouse? Or is it exclusive merely because you have lowered your intimacy with everyone else? How is your marriage equation being balanced? By giving to your spouse or by taking away from others?

In miserable marriages, if there is any exclusivity, it exists solely as the result of the latter. This is especially common in abusive and domination-based marriages. This scenario occurs often. An abusive husband demands exclusivity from his wife. The broken wife, unable to increase her intimacy with her husband, attempts to appease her spouse by withdrawing from everyone else. The end result is certainly exclusivity, though it is also misery.

So do you promote your spouse or demote others?

In healthy marriages, the answer is always "both." People in great marriages continually elevate their spouses' roles in their lives. They seek ever deeper, exclusive connections. At the same time, they also continually temper the levels of intimacy that they share with others, ensuring that those relationships never exceed the intimacy they share with their spouse. With regard to giving their spouses exclusivity, they know no bounds. But when it comes to limiting the intimacy they share with others, they always seek healthy moderation.

Marital exclusivity is all in the eyes of the beholder. In this case, the beholder is your spouse, your mirror. Because of the subjective nature of all of this, it's pointless to try to objectively prove whether or not your spouse feels that they have exclusive intimacy with you in all aspects of your life. It is completely irrelevant whether or not you can factually prove that you are more invested in your relationship with your spouse than you are in your relationship with your buddies or coworkers or parents or anyone else.

Your spouse's feelings are all that matter. If your spouse doesn't feel that they are your utmost interest, concern, and passion, nothing else matters. In this regard, their perception is the only truth. Perception is absolutely reality, as long as it is your spouse's perception and not yours.

Even if you disagree with your spouse's perception, you must accept that it is their perception. His or her entire worldview flows from that perception. Assuming he or she is being honest with you, their perspective is their reality. It's their truth. Denying their truth will prevent you from understanding their position.

If a wife tells her husband that she feels as though his business partner has taken her place as his highest priority, no amount of explanation, rationalization, or debate will improve the situation. The only positive resolution requires that he accept her perception as being her truth. His wife needs to have her grievance accepted. She then deserves to have her assurances restored. Her husband, even if he disagrees with his wife's complaint, needs to take immediate and overt actions to both elevate his intimacy with his wife and temper his relationship with his business partner. Whether this means checking in on his wife during his business day, refusing to allow his business partner's emails to interrupt his family's dinners, or any other measure, he should do it. When his wife's sense of exclusivity is restored, then she will once again feel the fullness of what it is to be married.

Tom was deeply involved in his church. He had a burning

desire to witness to lost souls and bring them into God's saving grace. So, he signed up for every outreach program his church offered. If there were doors to knock, homeless folks to feed, altar calls to participate in, baptisms to perform, tracts to be passed out, or special services to prepare for, he was there, enthusiastically.

Tom was also married to Cheryl. (Actually, Tom still is married to Cheryl, but he also was married to her several years ago when this situation took place.)

At least once a week and often more, Tom would meet with members of his church, and they would minister to the unconverted. They did everything they could to reach unchurched souls. And, to their credit, some people even became believers.

Cheryl stayed at home. She didn't do this because she didn't want to join Tom. She simply couldn't. They had children. They had a house to clean and grass to mow. They had other commitments. She tended to those.

As the months wore on, Tom and Cheryl's marriage began to suffer. Tom's ministry became increasingly demanding of his time and focus. Souls were hanging in the balance, and he felt that he had to act — even if that meant forgoing a date night or coming home too tired to invest any energy into whatever interested Cheryl. As much as he wanted to be there for Cheryl, hell burned hot and Tom felt that he had no choice but to look beyond their immediate lives and focus on saving eternal lives.

Meanwhile, Cheryl began to resent Tom. Petty things that he did began to annoy her. Likewise, Tom also began to feel unappreciated by Cheryl. He felt that she wasn't supporting him the way a wife should (in ministry, no less). Their feelings festered.

Tom and Cheryl's situation is very common, though the

contributing factors aren't always so highly spiritualized. Sure, Tom was doing good. In fact, Tom was doing wonderful, eternal, world-changing things. So how could Tom's good deeds have caused such a rift in their marriage? Aren't blessings supposed to follow those who bless others and do the will of God? How could Tom's good deeds have been so negatively reflected by his wife? Furthermore, why was Tom producing resentment in Cheryl?

Remember, the mirror can only reflect what it is given. The mirror should not be blamed.

By making his ministry efforts his foremost priority, passion, and interest, Tom essentially demoted his wife to second-class status.

Tom didn't put Cheryl first.

Because Cheryl wasn't assured of her place as Tom's highest priority, insecurities abounded. She became justifiably jealous of Tom's misdirected passion for the wellbeing of other people. Whether or not she even realized it, Cheryl felt contempt toward Tom's new mistress, Evangelism.

As Tom's mirror, Cheryl's discontent exposed the misalignment of Tom's priorities. Sure, *what* Tom was doing was good. However, *how* he did it was inappropriate, given the context of his marriage.

And so it is with countless other couples. They let other things and other people, become their top priorities. Poker nights. Church. School. The kids. Careers. Financial security. Anything that you invest your life into, if left unchecked, carries the risk of replacing your spouse as your highest priority. But nothing on this earth should ever come before your spouse.

In religious communities, people often make the mistake of elevating their religion ahead of their spouse. Pastors often neglect their families as they tend to their churches. Those in the congregation may sacrifice their marriages to support their religious leaders.

"I'm putting God first," they all theorize in an attempt to justify their actions. That, however, is untrue.

They aren't serving God. They're serving God's people. The distinction is important. When a pastor fails to spend time with his wife because he is hosting nightly dinners for the city's homeless men and women, he is letting those men and women take his wife's spot as his highest priority. It is unlikely that God has explicitly told him to neglect his marriage and devote his time in this manner. Even if God has asked him to feed the homeless, the pastor then has an obligation to figure out how to do so in a way that doesn't shirk his obligations toward his wife. When he's neglecting his wife, the pastor isn't serving God, even though he may be serving God's people. And, should his wife grow justifiably dissatisfied with her plight, she wouldn't be reacting against God's will.

Humans are spiritual beings. Men and women have intuition and responses that are triggered by the spirits of those around them. Nowhere is this more evident than within marriages. The challenge, however, is for one to become attuned the causes of his or her spouse's reactions.

Cheryl, like many (if not most) spouses, had no idea what was actually causing her contempt. She didn't realize that Tom's priorities were misaligned. When asked, she couldn't identify the core cause, so she blamed it on countless trivial matters. She never would have dreamed — let alone dared to say — that she was jealous of Tom's ministry. (After all, it was "for the Lord.") But that was exactly the subconscious source of her discontent. She was jealous, exactly as she should have been. Something had taken away what belonged to her: Tom's exclusivity. But her mind didn't realize it, even though her spirit felt the absence. Nevertheless, the inability to diagnose the cause of a problem doesn't make it any less of a problem.

Whether or not it's realized, the spirits of husbands and wives can serve to test their spouses' priorities. These tests can take many forms. For instance, a wife may make seemingly irrational demands, such as requiring her spouse to participate in ultimately meaningless activities. ("Can you go to the grocery store with me?") Or, she may ask him to make a sacrifice. ("Can you turn off that football game?" or "Can you freeze your shopping budget for a month?") Ultimately, it's not the end result of the action or inaction that matters. The goal isn't really to spend a finite amount of time or curb expenses. What actually matters is the response. It's a test. She is simply seeking to be reassured that other things have not risen to the level of becoming untouchable sacred cattle.

Fortunately, there is a solution. And Tom and Cheryl found that solution.

Before everything else that life may throw at you, you have to assure your spouse that they are, and will remain, your highest earthly priority. Your spouse must know, unequivocally, that he or she is exclusively yours and that your life is primarily committed to their good. This is best accomplished proactively — as opposed to reactively, only after the insecurities have already emerged. If your spouse is confident in their status as your foremost priority, the tests will cease. Trust will emerge. Freedom will follow.

In Tom's case, he withdrew from his ministry programs. Tom demoted evangelism. He centered his attention exclusively on increasing his intimacy with Cheryl. He focused on acing every test. It took some time, but eventually Cheryl became assured of her place as Tom's top priority. And, by serving his God-ordained spouse and fulfilling his vowed duties, Tom actually began truly serving the Lord.

Today, Cheryl has no doubt that she is Tom's foremost interest and passion. Because she is. Exclusively. Consequently, Tom is now more involved in evangelism than ever before, and Cheryl is fully supportive. She is no longer jealous of Tom's ministry efforts, because she knows that they are not taking anything from her. Cheryl knows that nothing else comes before her. Tom has no other loves before Cheryl.

Chapter Two
Thou shalt not make unto thee any graven image.

In light of the first commandment, "You shall have no other gods before me," this second commandment almost seems a bit redundant. Obviously, God didn't want His people to have other priorities, other lovers, other spouses. Marriages need exclusivity. This second commandment serves to reiterate that point, but it also adds a new layer of nuance to the marriage God wanted with His bride, Israel.

Throughout recorded history, many world religions have used sculptures and other material artifacts in their worship. From temples to personal homes, archaeologists and anthropologists around the world have discovered that the creation and ownership of religious icons has been a nearly universal human phenomenon. These figures range from tiny medallions to enormous statues and shrines, but they all serve the same purpose; they exist as stand-ins for supernatural beings.

Throughout many world religions, idols continue to be used as representations of gods, ancestors, and spirits that are otherwise not perceptible through human senses. These creations are then treated as surrogates for their respective otherworldly counterparts. As such, they are revered within their religions. When an idol is worshiped, it is thought that one is then vicariously worshiping the entity whom the idol represents. While idols are not — on their own — generally considered to be supernatural beings, they are considered to be representatives or substitutes for supernatural beings. Thus, the practice of idolatry isn't merely the creation or possession of various objects. Idolatry is, in fact, the use of surrogates.

In this second commandment, Yahweh told His bride that she had to refrain from practicing idolatry. While Egypt was full of idols, they were no longer in Egypt. That behavior couldn't continue if they were going to build a meaningful relationship with Him.

God didn't want anything to replace Him. Only Yahweh was to be their God. Only Yahweh could be the true spouse to His wife, Israel, and He didn't want to be replaced by a stand-in. He wasn't willing to have His relationship with Israel blocked by an intermediary figure. He wanted to represent Himself and for His bride to relate directly with Him. Given the finite nature of human imagination, any substitute, conjured up in the minds of men and women, would surely be a poor representation of an infinite God.

In the same way, the message of the second commandment is that husbands and wives need to be careful to refrain from making replacements for their spouses. Regardless of the form or function, nothing should substitute the roles within marriage. Husbands and wives absolutely must not let anything — or anyone — replace their spouses.

In the most immediate example, this certainly speaks to sexual substitutes. A mistress is a substitute for a wife. The sin of adultery, while a transgression in and of itself, also touches many other sins, including the act of idolatry, or illegitimate substitution. Thus, husbands and wives shouldn't physically or emotionally interact with anyone else as though they were their spouse. That's fairly obvious — important, but obvious.

This commandment, however, goes much deeper than mere physical substitutes. Just as almost anything can become a religious idol, so too can just about anything become a substitute for your spouse. And like religious idolatry, marital substitution is universal enough to be considered a plight of the fallen human condition. Husbands and wives are faced with inclinations and cultures that strongly (although often subconsciously) encourage the indulgence of spousal surrogacy. You must learn to resist that. Let only your spouse be your only spouse. No substitutes. Ever.

Building upon the first commandment, marital surrogates often violate the exclusivity that spouses owe to one another. In a recent study published by the National Bureau of Economic Research, economists John F. Helliwell, from the Vancouver School of Economics, and Shawn Grover, of the Canadian Department of Finance, evaluated the presence of happiness in the lives of married folks. Specifically, they examined levels of happiness throughout the course of peoples' lives. And they found some interesting truths.

For many years, a large body of research has continually demonstrated that people experience a U-curve of happiness throughout their lives. In their youth and senior years, people tend to report high levels of happiness, but that happiness tends to dip toward unhappiness during middle-age. This is often attributed to the stress produced by the demands of raising children and increased pressures in folks' careers. Midlife crises and declines in physical wellbeing are also common factors. However, while that U-curve is largely consistent throughout society, people who are married tend to experience higher highs and their low points are generally not as low as those who are unmarried.

Diving into this phenomenon even deeper, Helliwell and Grover discovered something important. They found that the positive effects of marriage on life satisfaction is greatly increased when a spouse regards their other half to be their best friend. And the difference was not a small margin either. They found that, for people who considered their spouses to be their best friends, the benefit of marriage on their life satisfaction actually doubled, when compared against those who were married but had best friends outside their marriages. So while marriage improves happiness throughout the lower points of the U-curve of lifelong satisfaction, being married to your best friend makes it even better.

But not everyone considers their spouse to be their best friend. Many people have substitutes filling that role. Statistically, women, more so than men, are apt to consider their best friend to be someone other than their spouse. This is particularly problematic because it is actually wives who experience the greatest benefit from being married to their best friends. As such, the very people who could receive the most advantageous results from marriage are also the most likely to miss out due to misplaced friendships.

Certainly, there are many factors that influence who one considers to be his or her closest friend. Perhaps the emotional absence of a husband causes his wife to seek intimate friendship with others. Or maybe, due to his interests and hobbies, a husband finds male companionship to be easier to obtain than close friendship with his wife. Regardless of the reason or excuse, even the secular research of Helliwell and Grover reinforces the truth that marriages are best when spouses regard one another as their exclusive best friend.

When spouses develop friendships with others — friends, family members, coworkers, etc. — that supersede the friendship shared within their marriage, they've created a substitute. Such substitutes undermine the health of a marriage because they take what rightfully belongs to one spouse and give it to another person. Furthermore, when a husband or wife derives the joy of the highest levels of friendship from someone other than their spouse, they are allowing that third party to act as their spouse, at least in regard to companionship. Therefore, the very act of nurturing a surrogate friendship — a friendship that exists outside of the marriage with the result of compensating for a deficit within one's spousal relationship — is actually an act of marital idolatry.

Paula and Bruce had three kids and a seemingly normal suburban life. Paula was a stay-at-home mom. Bruce worked long hours making other people rich. Their marriage was average, which is certainly not a compliment.

Because of Bruce's absence, Paula invested a tremendous amount of time building relationships with her children. In doing so, she hoped to make up for their uninvolved father. She constantly sought out wonderful experiences, from lavish vacations to extracurricular activities, which she shared with her children. Like many mothers, Paula considered her children to be her closest friends.

Eventually, Paula became dependent on her children. They became Paula's outlet for her social needs. They served as her companions and confidants. When she had a rough day, she relied on her children to be the source of her joy. In many respects, Paula used her children as substitutes for her husband.

Over time, this dependence grew. It eventually evolved to the point where Paula felt more committed to her children than she was to her husband. In fact, she felt that life was her and the kids versus her husband. Like all unhealthy dependencies, it had a debilitating effect on many aspects of Paula's life — not the least of which was her marriage.

For Paula, the substitute seemed to work, especially in the early stages. It helped her overcome her loneliness. Her substitution made her happy. It was like a drug for her. It got her through her days. But, like a drug, it eventually made her weaker. Her surrogate was never sufficient enough to fully meet her needs.

Paula's life is a common pattern. It manifests itself in countless ways, but the intent is generally the same. When people lack something in their lives, they seek substitutions. It's the same thing the Israelites did with the golden calf. When the Israelites didn't feel that Yahweh was tangible enough, they sought an alternative way to see and feel Him. They made a surrogate, an idol. The golden calf wasn't intended to be a different god. Quite the opposite, actually. It was created to represent Yahweh. The Israelites thought that by worshiping this stand-in, they could better worship God. They believed that their bovine surrogate would be an improvement to their divine relationship, as it would satiate their desire for a more overt sensory experience. They wanted to fill a void, to make up for something that they thought was lacking. They weren't satisfied with a spiritually omnipresent God. Instead, they wanted the security of something they could possess — something that could be physically present.

Idolatry is fundamentally rooted in insecurity. In every form, it's an attempt to forge a surrogate for something that's perceived to be missing. An idol is always a stand-in for the real thing.

In every culture throughout history, people have sensed the existence of higher powers. But they have often been discontent with divine authority that they could not see. So, people have made objects to serve as surrogates for the gods they could not behold.

They gave those gods names and tried to define their abilities and character. But they were never sufficient. Often, in experiencing the various facets of divinity, ancient cultures felt that it was necessary to then create additional idols to represent the components of otherworldly power that they had experienced. For instance, Zeus was thought to be the god of thunder and justice. But the ancient Greeks recognized that Zeus didn't capture the spiritual essence of love, so they also made Aphrodite. Pantheons were then built to represent the multitude of otherworldly powers that people perceived. And they were not exclusive. People worshiped many gods — each with their own particular set of believed powers, authority, personality, and agendas.

In the time of Moses, Scripture states that Pharaoh acknowledged the existence of Yahweh. The Egyptians were open to the idea of an unlimited number of gods. In fact, throughout their generations and regions, their pantheons changed over time. The Egyptians were willing to accept Yahweh as merely a part of their pantheon. Essentially, they thought of Yahweh as nothing more than yet another god in the universe. What they were not able to comprehend is that Yahweh was the true, comprehensive God and that their gods were merely misunderstandings of, and poor substitutes for, the true divine power.

The Egyptians were religiously insecure. They wanted gods that they could touch and see and own. An intangible God was too abstract for them, especially when He came at the cost of discarding their tangible idols. They preferred satisfying their insecurities to accepting the truth.

Often, marriages are the same.

Instead of acknowledging and embracing the roles, responsibilities, and realities of their marriages, people create surrogates. A husband, feeling familial insecurity due to his distant wife, may choose to overly invest his time by micromanaging the lives of his children. Likewise, a wife who feels emotionally unfulfilled may rely on her church to serve as a surrogate for her detached husband. Surrogates can come in many forms: friends, social functions, pornography, careers, drugs, spirituality, etc. Even the positive elements of life can become idols when they are used in attempts to satiate insecurities that should be satisfied and healed through one's spouse.

Ultimately, surrogates only serve to deepen such insecurities. Just as an idolatrous religion can keep a person from growing closer to Yahweh, so too can a spousal substitution keep one from finding security in their spouse. Remedying any insecurity requires three things: awareness, will, and effort. If temporary substitutes temporarily satiate one's insecurities, it becomes difficult — if not impossible — to achieve any of those three elements.

Awareness comes through honesty. When insecurity is satiated (instead of remedied), it becomes difficult to honestly assess one's feelings and present situation. A wife who feels insecure about her sexuality may allow erotic media (even pornography) to serve as a surrogate fix for her feelings. By vicariously experiencing sexual gratification through the lives of those in books and movies, she is able to gain a sense of sexual fulfillment without ever risking the vulnerability that comes through sharing true sexual intimacy with her husband. But, if her surrogate continually satiates her, she will never fully realize the depth of her own insecurity. She won't know what's missing. Her fake surrogate may cloud her ability to accurately examine and appraise her own condition and circumstance. Just as a doctor may carefully stress a condition to explore its severity and diagnose an ailment, sometimes it is necessary to experience some discomfort to properly evaluate the conditions of one's heart and mind.

Once a person is aware of his or her insecurity, they must then have the desire to improve. Will is essential. Without it, the understanding of one's own insecurity is futile. If the wife in this example doesn't want to find sexual security with her husband, the recognition of her substitution is ultimately pointless. She will simply return to her old ways or find a new surrogate. But, if she does want to remedy her sexual insecurity, she must then have the will to work toward building intimacy with her husband. She has to want her husband to be her husband, her exclusive intimate companion. With that desire, she can then take the steps that will lead her toward security. The process of change requires determination.

The journey toward security requires a tremendous amount of concerted effort. Building strength requires exercise. Likewise, the weakness of insecurity cannot be overcome apart from proactive action. This wife must purposefully engage in experiences that will negate her surrogate and build intimacy with her husband. She needs to identify and stop the moments when she utilizes and strengthens her surrogate. She needs to have naked conversations with herself and her husband (perhaps both literally and figuratively). By consciously revealing and exploring her thoughts, she can then create opportunities for trust to grow within her marriage. And trust leads directly to security.

Only your spouse should be your spouse. This means that you shouldn't seek substitutes to make up for the deficiencies that you see in your life or in your spouse. It also means that you shouldn't use other things to represent your spouse. For example, don't love your children because they remind you of your spouse. Love your children because they are your children, and love your spouse because he or she is your spouse. Likewise, if your spouse doesn't seem to meet your emotional or interpersonal needs, resist the inclination to find someone else to do just that.

Ultimately, if you believe that God has a plan and a purpose for your life, your spouse is part of that plan and purpose. You are married to your spouse for a reason, God's reason. To substitute what God has given you (your spouse) — on any level — is to avoid the opportunity that God has placed in your life. There is a reason. Don't miss it by pursuing substitutes.

Chapter Three
Thou shalt not take the name of the Lord, thy God, in vain.

This commandment is often misunderstood. Like many topics in Scripture, the third commandment has become somewhat of a hackneyed idea for many people. The assumptions of its intent are so commonplace, people often fail to fully understand it. Despite what your Sunday school teacher may have told you, this commandment doesn't really pertain to PG-13 references to God. It isn't merely God telling mankind not to mutter "Jesus" when they stub their toes in the dark, though that certainly is neither a proper nor a respectful response. No, it is much deeper.

When people get married, brides usually take their husband's last name. By carrying their respective husbands' surnames, brides signify that they are now functioning within covenants with their new husbands. This symbolic act shows that, together, their lives are now fused as one. They are no longer members of two separate families. They are now one unified family. Through this act, they establish a foundational expression of their covenant. The same thing happened within the marriage between Yahweh and His bride.

When the Israelites married God, they took on His name. They did so with an understanding of what His "name" actually meant. It wasn't merely a symbolic transfer of a surname — it was a covenantal extension of His power into their lives.

In Hebrew thought (and, consequently, in the minds of those who wrote the Bible), a "name," or *shem* in Hebrew, is synonymous with one's reputation and authority. It's the same idea carried by King Solomon when he said that a "good name" is better than material wealth. Solomon was talking about having a good reputation with the authority of strong personal integrity — not the merits of having a literal moniker that is cool (like "Solomon"). It was with that perspective that the Israelites understood this commandment. As they took on the name of God, they knew that they were now an extension of His authority and entwined in His reputation.

To understand the full, Biblical meaning of one's "name," it is helpful to think of it foremost in the context of reputation and authority. This concept gets clouded by modern connotations, through which a "name" is thought of primarily as one's appellation (their proper noun). This definition should be kept in check when studying the Hebraic text of the Bible. Instead, the primary definition of "name" should first be understood to refer to one's reputation and authority. An easy way of positioning one's understanding of this is to think of it in the same context used by Dianna Ross in the song "Stop in the Name of Love." In the song, the authority of love was used to appeal to the antagonist. A name isn't just a word — it represents the entirety of one's essence.

The understanding of the full weight of this concept exposes tremendous layers of meaning to Scripture, especially as it pertains to the nature of God and His relationship with humanity. For instance, when Moses encountered Yahweh in the form of a burning bush, Moses was worried that the Israelites would doubt his credibility and ability to lead them out of slavery. Moses was afraid that the Israelites would question God's role in their impending revolution by asking, "What is His name?" It wasn't that the Israelites would want to know the identity of God — that had already been addressed. Instead, it was that they would wonder whose authority was going to free them from the authority of Pharaoh. Likewise, the book of Philippians states that under the authority ("name") of the Messiah, "every knee shall bow." In 2 Samuel it is written that the reputation ("name") of God will be "magnified forever." In 1 Chronicles, King David spoke under the authority ("name") of the Lord. And the Psalms are filled with references to Yahweh's authority ("name") producing safety and His reputation (again, "name") being worthy of praise. It's not merely about the letters of His literal name. It's foremost about the fame and power of Yahweh. This cannot be overstated.

Throughout history, humans have often harmed God's name. Even His own bride has a spotted past with regard to bearing His reputation. The Israelites often failed to portray Yahweh in a positive light. Likewise, to this day, believers often drive folks away from God by misrepresenting who He is. In many circles, the actions of the Church have tragically made God infamous and caused many to deny His existence. ("If these Christians represent the nature of their God, I don't want anything to do with Him," many atheists surmise.) Due to misrepresentations of God, His own bride has caused many people to quite literally regard Yahweh as vanity, empty nothingness. The bride has carried His name in vain.

By joining in a covenant with humanity, God opened Himself up to the risk of having His reputation harmed. But such risk is necessary within marriage, as it is within any covenant. Yahweh knew that by entering into this covenant He would be known as Israel's God. His honor would be tied to the reputation of His bride. Yahweh could have had exclusivity with Israel without entrusting His reputation to her. He could have also demanded that she not create substitutes for him without binding His reputation to her. He could have done many things and kept His reputation to Himself. But that wouldn't have been a covenant. Covenants require vulnerability. When two parties are bound together, they both become susceptible to the risk of having their reputations compromised. A covenant joins the two parties as one, intrinsically intertwining their honor and fame.

History fondly remembers Coretta Scott King, foremost because she bore her husband's reputation, through which she was able to make great strides on behalf of her nation. On the opposite end of the spectrum, Eva Braun will always be remembered with contempt and infamy due to her husband's reputation. Both women, as with all spouses, were tied to the reputations of their spouses. One is highly regarded for advancing the work of Dr. Martin Luther King, Jr., and the other is derided as the cohort of Adolf Hitler. In Eva's case, her spouse absolutely violated the principle of the third commandment by destroying her "name" through his actions. Whatever trust she extended to him certainly did not work toward her benefit.

The union of two entities comes with the potential for hazards. That risk only increases as the character of the individuals declines. When a man and woman enter into a covenant, they are binding their lives and their reputations together. Their fates become intertwined, which can both increase the heights of success and deepen the valleys of failure.

All partnerships are inherently risky. The risk of going into business with someone opens the door for that other person to harm your reputation. When two nations enter into a trade agreement, the benefits of doing so are only possible if they are willing to accept the risk that one nation might betray the other. Likewise, when a man and a woman agree to forge a lifelong partnership through the covenant of marriage, they become vulnerable to the risk that they may be betrayed. And specific to the third commandant, is the risk that such betrayal may harm one's reputation. Yahweh's prohibition against having His name misused speaks to the risk and weight of responsibility that exists within the partnership of marriage.

Marriage makes one vulnerable, but it also allows both parties to experience the benefits of having a partner upon whom they can rely. When a husband entrusts his wife with all aspects of his life, including his reputation and authority, it allows him to rest in the security of knowing that someone else is looking after his best interest and is standing beside him to assist him through life. When a wife extends the same trust to her husband, she also experiences the peace that comes from having a partner with whom she can share the joys and withstand the hardships of life. Nevertheless, both are only able to receive the benefits if they are also willing to accept the risk inherent in their covenant. Likewise, Yahweh's partnership with Israel, though it exposed His name to risk, served to benefit both parties. By forging a covenant-based relationship, Yahweh received worship, Israel received God's blessings, and both received an everlasting relationship.

Like much of Scripture, the full implications of the third commandment are widespread. To begin to scratch the surface, one must understand the breadth of meaning in the words that comprised the commandment. It's rooted in understanding the concept of one's name, but it doesn't stop there.

The prohibited verb (or action) of the third commandment is often translated in English as "take." In the original Hebrew, this word means "carry." Therefore, it should be understood that what the commandment forbids is to take on, or carry, the authority and reputation of God in vain. At Sinai, during the Israelites' marriage to Yahweh, this was particularly profound. In the very moment that they were taking on, or beginning to carry, the name of God, Yahweh was telling them to do so with intention and care: "Do not carry My name in vain."

In the same manner, a husband and wife should approach their marriage with gravity. They should fully appreciate and respect their covenant. Through marriage, they carry one another's reputation and authority. This is not something that should be taken lightly. Marriages shouldn't be entered into casually, and they certainly shouldn't be lived out with reckless disregard.

In the commandment, coupled with the concept of carrying someone's reputation and authority, is the idea of doing something "in vain." It also deserves examination. When it is said that someone is "vain" (which is surely the most common context of that word), what is meant is that there is a selfish meaningless to their actions or attitudes. Vanity, reduced to its most base definition, is emptiness, worthlessness. Therefore, in this commandment there is a prohibition against entering the covenant and bearing Yahweh's reputation and authority in an empty, meaningless way.

By marrying Israel, Yahweh was entrusting His name to His bride. Likewise, when a man and woman marry, they are conferring their reputations and authority to one another. How they use that power has a tremendous impact on the strength of their marriage. If they use their covenant and one another's reputation and authority for selfish, worthless purposes, they are guilty of violating the principle of the third commandment.

Ultimately, in a marriage, both spouses continually represent one another's reputations and bear the authority of each other. As a spouse, you do not act alone. Who you are and what you do will have a direct impact on your spouse's authority and reputation. Don't bear their name in vain.

CHAPTER THREE

Phillip and Peggy were at a moment of marital crisis. Things had gone from mediocre to terrible over the course of their six-year marriage. Both of them were unhappy, and divorce had become a serious thought in their minds.

When asked what was causing them so much grief, their answers were a laundry list of petty complaints. Phillip didn't like how Peggy managed money. Peggy thought Phillip was spending his time poorly. They both thought each other were wasting their potential and undermining the future of their family. They both were annoyed by one another's habits and interests. It was fairly common stuff. No big sins. No affairs. Just a general dislike for how both of them were choosing to live their lives.

What it really came down to was a lack of trust. Distrust. Both Phillip and Peggy distrusted how each other made decisions. Phillip felt that Peggy's free-spending ways were irresponsible and holding their family back from being able to have his desired degree of financial security. He wanted them to share a greater sense of self-determination — a form of authority — over their economic status, but he felt that his wife was working against that goal. At the same time, Peggy felt that Phillip's hobbies and social activities, which generally revolved around video games and NASCAR, monopolized his time and showed immaturity and a lack of healthy priorities. Peggy wanted their family to build a reputation as positive role models for, and active participants in, their social circles and community, but she felt that Phillip was an obstacle to that end.

They were both right.

The problem, though, was they both felt they could operate in a vacuum. They didn't realize that their choices were having an impact on one another's sense of authority and perception of his or her reputation. They were — in completely separate ways — making each other feel that their reputations and authority were wasting away.

Peggy's fiscal indulgences left Phillip feeling continually as though they were behind the eight ball financially. There were things that he wanted to do for their family's long-term economic security, but he couldn't because there always seemed to be "too much month at the end of the money." He wasn't worried about keeping up with the Joneses so much as keeping ahead of the repo man.

At same time, Phillip's activities monopolized his time to the extent that he (and often Peggy, as well) was unable to participate in opportunities that could have enhanced their lives together. For instance, because of Phillip's recreational activities, they were routinely unable to participate in functions at their church. Peggy also wanted them to volunteer in various charitable and community activities, but she was held back by Phillip's lack of availability. This often left Peggy feeling unfulfilled and, frankly, embarrassed.

They failed to realize that, in a marriage, one's actions are not individual actions. All actions have the potential to affect both parties. What one spouse does can — and generally does — have a direct impact on the other spouse's sense of his or her own reputation and authority.

Phillip and Peggy both felt that the other was undermining their collective success. That feeling was accurate. As bearers of each other's names, they were reckless and irresponsible. Through their individual actions, they were eroding one another's names. Phillip's actions limited the reputation of their family. At the same time, Peggy's choices had diminished Phillip's authority over important aspects of his life. Both felt the sting of waning potential. Ultimately, because they were not confident in each other's competence to make "the right" decisions, doubt crept in. Trust was lost. And without trust, relationships fail.

There is yet another level of meaning to this commandment. The commandment, "Do not take My name in vain," bears a stark instruction. As this is the outset of a covenant in which Yahweh's name would be conferred to His bride, one can conclude that this is actually an instruction for the Israelites to enter the covenant seeking purposeful substance. To avoid violating the prohibition, the Israelites had to accept this covenant with the full intent of having a meaningful relationship with God. Put in modern terms, this commandment could be phrased, "Do not take on this covenant for nothing."

When a man and woman marry, they are given the same charge. In taking on one another's names, they should be intentional about making their union one of value. Marriage is not simply an arrangement. It is a lifelong covenant. The failure to consider the gravity and ramifications of one's marriage is a failure to uphold the principle of the third commandment.

Many marriages fail because their covenants — the very foundations of their marriages — were made in vain. People often commit perjury toward God by professing undying commitment toward their spouses during their wedding vows, while maintaining thoughts of self-serving opportunism: "If this doesn't work out and I'm not happy, we'll just get divorced," they tell themselves. Instead of fully committing to their marriages, they half-heartedly enter into their covenants, knowing that they are not truly committed to a sincere, lifelong promise. As such, their very vows are made in vain. They are empty and meaningless. And so, their marriages often follow suit.

Bearing an empty covenant is not limited merely to the day

the vows are said. Many marriages suffer from the same emptiness. Often, though the vows may have been made with full sincerity, the weight of subsequent years can press the intentionality out of a marriage. Spouses lose sight of the worth of one another and the value of their marriage. Their covenants become, functionally, in vain.

Since the prohibition of the third commandment includes bearing the covenant without meaningful intentionality, husbands and wives should likewise be purposefully deliberate in their own marriages. Their marriages should be meaningful and make a difference — both to them as individuals and from them as a unified name.

The state of being married should produce opportunities to add worth to one's spouse. Through the intentional commitment of your life to your spouse, you should continually strive to increase his or her value. Your marriage shouldn't result in their emptiness. Your vanity shouldn't cause them to live in vain. Remember, the opposite of vanity (empty worthlessness) is fullness and worth. Your marriage should fill your spouse's life with richness.

Together, the union shared by you and your spouse should increase the reputation and authority of your lives. The fact that you are married to your spouse should have a positive impact on those around you. If your marriage is healthy, your role in your spouse's life will result in your spouse's name being strengthened and elevated. Their efficacy and influence with others will increase as the result of your good marriage. This can materialize in many ways. For some, the goodness of their spouse improves their standing in their community. This is seen often with public figures and in religious communities. A good First Lady says a lot about the quality of her husband, and vice versa when the roles are switched. For others, their healthy marriages factor into their socioeconomic status and perceived competence and character. (Divorces are expensive and often carry the unfortunate social stigma of questioned character, regardless of the validity of such suspicions.) And there are countless other social ramifications that hinge on the strength of your marriage. As such, it is essential to be intentional about the success of your marriage, because the impact will exceed the scope of your individual life.

God designed the world as a place wherein increase is the fundamental result of healthy life. Seeds grow. Babies are born. Wealth is created. Populations increase. All of this is how the world is supposed to work. The increase of fullness and worth is the natural course of healthy life. Likewise, if your marriage is healthy, increase will be the natural result — even though it may come in forms as varied as the men and women who choose to marry. For instance, marriages often produce environments wherein couples can safely make babies and raise children. Likewise, many couples find that their marriages provide them with tactical support that empowers them to accomplish more with their lives than they would have been able to achieve otherwise. And while such external benefits are wonderful, healthy marriages also yield immense internal rewards. A husband's or wife's own sense of self-worth can be profoundly increased when they know that they are truly loved, wholly respected, and deeply valued by their spouse. Through purposeful intent, healthy marriages thwart emptiness by increasing the richness of life.

By making the commitment of being in covenant with your spouse, you should embrace the obligation to add value to their life. Your marriage should produce fullness through intentional decisions and actions. You should not carry your spouse's name in vain.

Chapter Four
Remember the Sabbath day to keep it holy.

The Sabbath is an interesting concept. Essentially, it's a weekly holiday. Of all the Ten Commandments, the fourth commandment is the only one where God explicitly tells His bride to participate in an activity. Essentially, Yahweh created the Sabbath as a day when His bride could, should, and would drop everything else and focus on Him.

Throughout the Bible, the Sabbath is described as a "sign" of Yahweh's marriage covenant with Israel. In the book of Ezekiel, for instance, Yahweh says that the Israelites broke their covenant with Him when they failed to uphold the Sabbath, "the sign between Me and them." The Sabbath was the primary thing that signified that they were His. And it was more than just a symbol.

God's marriage to Israel was represented by an activity.

In the book of Leviticus, Yahweh expounds on the fourth commandment. Fleshing out His intent and expectation regarding this aspect of Israel's relationship with Him, God says that the seventh day of the week is to be a "holy convocation." Restated, the

Sabbath was to be a dedicated gathering that happened on a weekly basis. Yahweh wanted His bride to come together, to be wholly present. And He wanted her to dedicate that time of wholeness to Him and to their relationship. The Sabbath was a time when Yahweh and Israel could be united and He could have her undivided attention. But it wasn't for Him. It was for her. In the passage from Ezekiel, Yahweh says He gave the Israelites the Sabbath "so that they might know that I am Yahweh who sanctifies them." The Sabbath was the way that Yahweh intended to let His bride know that she belonged to Him.

William and Shauna were busy people. They had kids, careers, and a crisis. Their marriage, like an airplane without fuel, had stalled and was in a free fall. Neither felt "in love." The fire had gone out. The spark was gone. All they had left was smoke and ashes, after years of having not refueled their marital fire.

The fascinating thing about William and Shauna is that they were both wonderful people. They loved each other. Deeply. They were kind, diligent, fun, and charitable. To all outside eyes, they appeared to have it all and have it together. They were role models for many people, including those in their church.

But they felt empty. Drained and dry.

Throughout the course of their busy lives, William and Shauna had failed to remember to keep a "Sabbath" in their marriage. They were never alone together in waking hours. Their children, friends, and colleagues were seemingly constant fixtures in their lives. Their sexuality suffered. Sex had become a chore that was always easier to just put off to another day. In the rare moments when they did find sufficient time, energy, and interest (or a sense of obligation) to bed one another, they often failed to be wholly present; their minds and hearts were often elsewhere. They didn't date each other. Nor did they strive to impress or please one another. They didn't set aside time to focus on simply talking with one another about their goals, hopes, fears, and interests. They were so caught up in the frenzy of their day-to-day lives that they never seemed able to find time to dedicate themselves to the activity of reconnecting with one another.

Over time, their lack of moments of intentional reconnection left them feeling disconnected. Yet they were oblivious to this obvious cause of their discontent. Like many couples, they couldn't put their finger on why they felt detached. They missed the simple truth: The remedy for feelings of disconnection is to connect, and "to connect" is a verb.

The Sabbath is an activity.

The Sabbath is an activity.

It's worth repeating because it is so fundamental to understanding what it is that marriages need: active participation. Too often, marriages suffer when spouses begin to take passive roles in their marriages. They put their marriages on autopilot and focus their energy, creativity, and passion elsewhere. This inevitably leads to disaster.

For a marriage to thrive, both spouses need to make a commitment to continually reconnect. And it has to involve activity. Connecting involves action. Inactivity and passivity will never lead to marital success, because one cannot connect without doing something. What that something is, can vary between couples, depending on their personalities, stages in life, and many other factors. Nevertheless, regardless of what action is taken, reconnecting should be a conscious, deliberate act. In the same way that observing the Lord's Day requires awareness, planning, and doing, a great marriage is built through intentional actions.

Focus on your spouse with your whole, undivided attention. Set aside time to do the action of reconnecting. That time should happen often. The more often, the better.

For some, a healthy step forward may be as simple as committing to the now cliché — through rarely practiced — weekly date night: a literal, weekly Sabbath of sorts. That's certainly a good place to start, though it should never become the exclusive time of active reconnection. Just as believers are able to commune with God, both continually and on a weekly basis, spouses too should seek to perpetually identify and pursue intentional moments of reconnection with one another.

When was the last time you played a game with just your spouse? (No, not a mental game — a literal game.) Odds are that it has been too long. So dust off the checkers and get busy "kinging" each other. It may sound juvenile, but even an act this simple will tell your spouse that you enjoy them, that you want to spend time with them, and that they are special. It builds your sense of companionship and creates opportunities for open communication.

You should identify opportunities to actively reunite. Ideally, these opportunities should happen on every level. Find ways to reconnect spiritually. Seek out things that will pull you closer together intellectually. Set aside time to be companions and reconnect as friends. Build something together — literally. Read a book together — out loud. Whatever you choose to do, you should focus on using that time as a means to get to the true end: drawing closer with your spouse.

Get physical and make love.

Throughout the Bible, there are widely ranging examples of weddings, but one thing is always consistent: Sex is what makes married people, in fact, married. Sexual activity is the most universal and authentic expression of marital togetherness. It's how marriages are "consummated," or completed. As such, sex can be one of the most powerful ways that a husbands and wives can build emotional unity. When couples fail to reconnect sexually, they functionally deny the very core of what it means to be married. Sex is the most literal way in which husbands and wives are able to reconnect.

On a chemical level, sex bonds people together. Throughout the last century, scientists have explored and begun to discover the ways in which sex alters one's feelings toward their partner. During sex, and particularly during orgasm, the human body releases oxytocin. This chemical is known as the "bonding hormone" due to its incredible ability to cause people to feel emotionally connected to one another. Sex also produces vasopressin and endorphins, which produce feelings of well-being and provide a chemical incentive for reconnection.

Ultimately, when you become diligent about keeping and protecting the Sabbaths of your marriage, you too will realize what the writers of the Bible meant when they described the Sabbath as a "sign." Your commitment to your spouse is signified by your purposeful participation in the activity of reconnection. It shows to your spouse (and those around you) that you are actively engaged in your marriage. This sign of active engagement is a factor that is missing in nearly all failing marriages.

So, get active. Remain active. Remember the Sabbath. Keep it.

But what if your Sabbath doesn't feel special? What if the "sign" feels more like a warning sign? What if spending time with your spouse feels more like a chore than a blessing?

Do it anyway.

Using Yahweh's commandment as an outline for the qualities that should be pursued in human marriages, one can see the necessity of this reconnection. God's Sabbath with Israel wasn't optional. It was a commandment. Essentially, God told His bride, "Even if you don't want to — even if you'd rather do something else — I insist that you come back to me." Granted, Yahweh didn't physically force the Israelites to participate. He did, however, clearly outline His expectation. Yahweh informed the Israelites that their relationship's success would be contingent on whether or not they would choose to engage in purposeful reconnection. If they wanted to continue their relationship, they needed to participate. There was no way around this. It was essential to their divine marriage.

However, years later, the Israelites stopped keeping their Sabbaths with Yahweh. (This is what the book of Ezekiel details.) Israel found new lovers. This led to God's separation from His bride, Israel. Failure to keep the Sabbath — to wholly reconnect — was a failure to keep the marriage.

Don't make the same mistake.

A marriage cannot survive without continued reconnection. Moments of reconnection — even moments that may seem to be less than what you may selfishly desire — will ultimately help preserve your marriage. For many, these Sabbaths are a new way of life. They require thoughts, plans, and actions that were previously non-existent. But, like other parts of your lifestyle, you too can develop the tendency to keep the Sabbaths of your marriage. It starts as tasks, which then become habits. Habits, when maintained over time, eventually internalize and become lifestyles and character traits. When it comes to your marriage, your Sabbaths are definitely worth cultivating and protecting.

When Yahweh gave the Lord's Day to His bride, He did so for her benefit. Christ emphasized this when He told the Pharisees that "the Sabbath was made for humans." Humans weren't created just to fit into some sort of divine weekly schedule simply to please God. In this truth, Christ revealed that God's institution of the fourth commandment was intended for the sole benefit of His bride. Likewise, it is important to remember that the Sabbaths of your marriage are not for you — they are for your spouse. Your intentional activities of reconnection should serve to reassure your spouse of his or her role in your life. Even though you both will participate, your goal should be to strengthen your spouse's awareness of your marriage covenant. Merely doing things together isn't enough. You should seek to highlight the things that signify your union.

And the opposite is also true. As you pursue times of reconnection, you should avoid activities that may cloud your spouse's perception of your marital bond or their role in your life. Attending strip clubs or swingers resorts together (admittedly, extreme examples) will not strengthen your marriage, despite the quantity of time spent in near proximity to one another. Why? It's simply because such adulterous settings decrease the reality of your spouse being your spouse, your exclusive sexual interest and partner. Likewise, while touring a brewery with an alcoholic spouse is probably not a good choice, treating that same spouse to a weekend getaway may lead to a perfect time of reconnection. Just as Yahweh desired for the Israelite's Sabbaths to revolve around the sacred religion that He established, so too should your marriage's Sabbatical activities align with the nobler interests of your spouse.

Your goal should always be to continually nurture and increase your spouse's sense of connection, both to you and to your marriage. Your unending mission should be to assure them of their true value and role within your life. Once you are cognizant of your spouse's feelings of connection or disconnection, then you can begin the process of establishing a pattern of actions that will — over time

— further unite you and your spouse. This connection must be an extension of your wholly devoted, perpetual focus. It absolutely must be a continual effort. At all times, you should strive to find ways to reconnect with your spouse. Though it may feel unnatural at first, always remember that you are building new habits. You are reprogramming your mind. A series of small actions, which may seem insignificant individually, will eventually develop a disposition and a lifestyle that is centered on marital connection. And a connected marriage is a happy marriage.

Chapter Five
Honor thy father and thy mother.

Honor is a rarity in modern society. Modern culture is permeated with the toxic air of casual indifference. People get a thrill out of disrespecting authority. They openly slander and disrespect national leaders. The public enjoys seeing celebrities' lives spin out of control. When pastors make mistakes, folks devour every delicious drop of salty gossip.

A simple glance at the covers of current tabloid magazines (which are designed precisely to be impulsively appealing) clearly demonstrates that human nature relishes in the disgrace of others. Publishers use the least flattering photos, the most shameful headlines, and the worst possible allegations to adorn their magazines' covers. All of this is intended for a single purpose; they want you to buy their magazines. They know that somewhere deep in humanity's basest nature is a desire to wallow in the dishonor of others. People enjoy seeing others be shamed. Sadly, men and women find sinful pleasure in the degradation of others. That fallen aspect of the human condition is why such publications exist.

In modern culture, honor seems to be a forgotten virtue. There was once a time when men honored the presence of women; if a female walked into the room, all men rose to their feet. There was a time when people dressed in their finest clothing just to go to church. It was a way in which they honored the presence of God, the work of the ministry, and the sanctity of the congregation. For many millennia, husbands would literally fight those who spoke against the honor of their wives. Back then, marriage meant something.

Could it be more than a coincidence that, as society has grown increasing dishonorable, the rate of divorce has risen exponentially?

Honor is a tricky concept for people to understand because it is so foreign to the modern western culture. On one hand, one is taught that honor is inherent in certain roles, positions, and people. On the other hand, folks also believe that honor should be earned. However, it's a mistake to think that these are conflicting opinions. It's a false dichotomy. Both options are true.

Yes, honor is inherently deserved. You should honor your spouse simply because he or she is your spouse. In some ways, this is actually a form of self-honor, as you are honoring the role that your spouse plays in your life. (And dishonoring your spouse is actually dishonoring yourself, which creates a vicious circle within which it is difficult to rebuild self-honor.)

And, yes, it is also true that honor is best when it is earned. When honor is earned, it flows freely and effortlessly. It's a natural result that produces love, respect, and joy. This truth, however, does not negate the previous paragraph. Even if honor is not earned, it should still be given, because it is still inherently due. It is still owed. Your spouse is honorable by virtue of your role in his or her life (as opposed to his or her role in your life).

Perhaps this is easier understood by taking it out of the context of a marriage. In the interest of highlighting this truth, let's look

CHAPTER FIVE

at a group of people that almost everyone loves to hate: politicians.

In the United States of America, there is a president. Regardless of their feelings toward the president, Americans should honor him or her because he or she is the president of their nation. This is not the same as honoring a president because of his or her platforms, actions, or anything he or she may have done to earn such honor. Whether or not the president ever *earns* the respect of the American people, the public should still extend honor toward their president simply because he or she is *their* president. There is honor in the role because it is an extension of the American public. As members of that citizenry, Americans cannot dishonor their president without dishonoring themselves. If for no other reason, they ought to recognize that their president bears honor by virtue of the fact that he or she represents them. Even if the president's only perceived merit is that the president represents one's own self, that alone should be enough to warrant the gift of honor.

Likewise, if for no other reason, a husband should honor his wife because she is his wife, regardless of whether or not he feels that she has done enough to "earn" his respect. Naturally, the same is also true of a wife toward her husband. Your spouse's honorability is, at least in part, the result of both their role *and* your role in their life. They are honorable because you are worthy of honor. And vice versa. It's a virtuous circle.

"Evidently, golf is more important than spending time with his children."

"Husbands can be so frustrating and immature."

"I can't believe that anyone could be this stupid."

On and on the posts went. For hours on end, Louisa told the world about the allegedly miserable man that she had the misfortune of marrying. She had a keyboard and WiFi, and she wasn't afraid to use them as she waged war against her husband.

On a golf course on the other side of town, Tony's phone kept alerting him to his wife's furry. With every notification, his love for his wife faded. By the time he got to the back nine, he wasn't sure what he hated more: His wife or himself for marrying her. He was sure of only two things: He was going to divorce Louisa, and he wasn't going home that night.

In the fifth commandment, God instructs His bride to honor her father and her mother. Like all of the commandments, this seemingly simple commandment is laced with many layers of complexity, each revealing more of the Father's intent. At its most fundamental level, this commandment demands that one honor his or her parents. Beyond just the literal mission of doing well by one's mom and dad, there is an obvious extension.

Parents are the most immediate and universal symbols of human authority. When Yahweh is described as "God Almighty" (*El Shaddai*, in Hebrew) in the Old Testament, that phrase is actually tied to the Hebrew words for both destruction, *shadad*, and the female breast, *shad*. Thus, while the imagery is certainly one of warlike power, it is tempered by the softer (albeit perhaps more absolute) power that a mother has over her newborn child. In this way, even the power of God is laced with connotations of maternal, parental authority. Throughout Scripture, the authority of parents over their children is symbolic of true authority. With this understanding, it is then logical to extend the scope of the fifth commandment and find additional meaning.

More than just a demand for the Israelites to honor their individual parents, the fifth commandment compelled the Israelites to extend honor to the authorities in their lives. It is the foundation upon which Yahweh expected His bride to build a culture of respect. For example, thousands of years later, building upon this very principle, the Apostle Paul advises for the believers in Rome to honor and show respect toward their secular government officials. There and elsewhere in the Bible, are instructions and examples that stem from this basic concept of showing honor to whom it is due.

Filial respect has been an inherent part of moral codes (including world religions) throughout history. The act of children showing honor toward their parents is a universal virtue. This has been such a widespread cultural expectation that it saturates many belief systems. An example of this is found in the philosophy of Confucius. Even though he died five centuries before the time of the Gospels, lived in China, and was generally removed from the teachings of the Israelite religion, he recognized the importance of familial honor. In fact, he even based his entire moral system entirely on the concept of parental authority. And in that regard, Confucius understood a deeper truth; filial respect is a baseline against which one's honor can be evaluated.

The fifth commandment is God's simple instruction for His bride to honor those in authority in her life. Obviously, this falls in line with the first commandment, which states that God is the highest authority. Both the first and fifth commandments require that honor be given to whom it is due.

In your marriage, your honor is due to your spouse.

In the previous story, Louisa dishonored Tony in a very public way. Tony also failed to honor Louisa by putting her first and skipping the links that afternoon. Their crisis that day was the boiling over of feelings of disrespect that had stewed for years. Their mutual failure to show honor, both interpersonally and publicly, ended their marriage.

Dishonor is poison to relationships. Fortunately, the opposite is also true; honor heals, strengthens, and empowers marriages.

Failing marriages are almost universally fraught with incidents of dishonor. These marriages are plagued with moments when spouses are shamed or disrespected before family and friends. Such marriages are also often spotted with moments when one spouse's feelings or opinions are ignored, dismissed, or belittled by the other spouse.

Conversely, great marriages are filled with honor. In a solid marriage, both spouses are universally eager to honor one another whenever the opportunity presents itself. Instead of discussing their spouse's mistakes, both sincerely praise the character, actions, and abilities of their spouse. When they interact with each other, they value one another's opinions. They seek their advice. They praise and never criticize.

Many authors and researchers have studied the impact of honor on marriage. Amid the extensive bibliographies available on this subject is the research published by Judith S. Wallerstein and Sandra Blakeslee. They studied and wrote about the lives of fifty happily married couples. As you might imagine, their findings (which were published in their book *The Good Marriage: How and Why Love Lasts*) found many common themes. Ultimately, they were able to place successful marriages into four distinct types, based on the dynamics of the relationships within the marriages. Even though they found a wide array of types of marital relationships, there was a common theme than ran through all of them: respect.

The fifty couples interviewed each described their respective marriages as being very happy. This happiness was tied to two important feelings. First, each spouse said they felt cherished and respected by their respective other half. Second, and perhaps more importantly, the husbands and wives all reported that they respected and admired certain qualities of their spouses. Thus, these husbands and wives felt honored by their spouses, and that feeling was rooted in the simple truth that their spouses actually felt they were married to honorable people. Imagine that. Their happy marriages were rooted in a symbiosis generated from accurate feelings of mutual respect and admiration.

Great marriages are those wherein both spouses actively convey and pursue a culture of honor. They feel that each other are honorable, and they feel honored. This symbiosis starts with the husband and the wife. (From there, it can then extend to their children, who reciprocate with filial respect.) Ultimately, it overflows into how they interact with everyone they encounter.

Honor isn't something that can be relegated to specific individuals. When you are honorable, it touches everyone. A true test of whether or not you are fully embracing honor can be found in how you regard those who are lower on your list of personal priorities, such as restaurant servers, employees, bosses, neighbors, those who are homeless, and others.

Many spouses feel that they behave honorably toward their other half, but their actions toward others reveal that they don't truly understand what it means to live honorably, living life with a predisposition for honor. One may praise his or her spouse but then rely on shame as a means of chastising their children. Perhaps a husband holds his family in high regard, but then gleefully slanders his community leaders. Or, maybe a wife thinks well of those in her religious community, but maliciously degrades her employees' sense of self-worth. Such actions reveal an ignorance of — or even contempt for — the value of true honor.

If honor is a virtue, then it must be extended to all and demonstrated toward all. Just as one cannot be truly kind without showing kindness to all, or truly humble without approaching every situation with humility, one cannot be honorable while dishonoring others. The virtue of honor must be universal. Anything less is hypocritical and merely a self-serving sham.

Ultimately, integrity is essential. If your acts of honor are only doled out to those who may benefit you, you are not wholly living a life of honor. What you are living is the life of a con man. You are manipulating your spouse (or others) for your own personal gain. You are pretending. You are going through the motions with neither sincerity nor integrity. And, in a marriage, your façade will eventually be revealed as insincere and a lie. To be worthy of honor and to truly show honor, you must be honorable.

When you are dishonorable, your lack of integrity impacts the life of your spouse and the health of your marriage. You must remember the role of your marital mirror, your spouse. The thing about a mirror is that it always shows the truth. Mirrors can only reveal what is placed before them. God has provided your spouse to you so that your true character can be revealed. When a wife shames her daughter into submission, or when a husband viciously attacks the reputation of a pastor, they can breed insecurity within their respective spouses. There isn't enough praise or kindness that can overcome the realization that one's spouse doesn't seek honor in others. That insecurity undermines the ability to feel confident in the honor being shown by one's spouse. In the back of their minds, those spouses are well aware of the fact that their husband or wife is inclined toward dishonor. And, it may be just a matter of time before those inclinations toward dishonor set their sights on them. At the very least, such moments of dishonor serve as a reminder of the emptiness of the "honor" their spouses have shown toward them.

George and Ruth were inseparable. They had been married for

decades, raised beautiful children, and spent a wonderful lifetime together. Their love was magnificent.

As the sun started to set on their lives, George began to suffer from Alzheimer's disease. At first, he would forget names and lose his train of thought mid-sentence. Over time, this grew more severe. Ultimately, like so many with this disease, he lost himself in thought more often than he found himself in life.

As George's mind faded, Ruth remained.

Every day, Ruth stayed by George's side. Through care centers, nursing homes, doctors' offices, and family gatherings, she remained a constant presence in his life, though she didn't have to do so. No one would have blamed Ruth if she had chosen to distance herself from George. Honestly, George wouldn't have even noticed if she left; he rarely noticed her when she was present. But she didn't walk away. She was always there to either try to talk him down from a tirade or talk him up to a stranger. She never wasted an opportunity to praise her husband for the man he once was and the man she knew him to be. Ruth refused to let others see him only as the man he had become. She talked about his accomplishments, his faith, and his character. She praised his love — even when it wasn't evident by his unintentional actions.

Though George's mind was departing, Ruth's heart was determined to not let his honor be diminished. George had always been her hero, and, during those final and difficult years, she felt that it was her opportunity to be his.

Instead of letting him fade into the darkness, Ruth fought for George's dignity and honor. Even in George's most troubled moments, Ruth remained sincere, loving, thankful, and full of grace. She knew that he was a man worthy of honor.

Ruth could have given up. She could have complained about the trials George had put her through. She could have quit. She didn't. In honoring her husband unto death, Ruth gained the honor of all who met her.

When George passed, the world lost a great man.

Later, when Ruth passed, the world lost a champion.

Chapter Six
Thou shalt not kill.

The sixth commandment starts a string of very blunt prohibitions. They seem so simple that it's easy to miss their full meaning. They almost seem like clichés. They're not. Given that these commandments pertain to both the spiritual and physical realms, you should search for meaning on multiple levels to fully grasp the deeper meaning behind these commandments.

As demonstrated in the previous chapters of this book, the literal meaning of Scripture is often a blueprint through which one can construct an understanding of much larger ideas. Additional layers of meaning build upon one another. Properly understood, they do not negate one another. Just as the fourth commandment ("Remember the Sabbath day") means to quite literally remember to practice a weekly day of rest *and also* conveys an underlying principle of seeking moments of intentional reconnection, every commandment carries multiple levels of meaning. Those levels of meaning are limitless, not merely confined to literal interpretations and marital advice. For many, it may be easy to extrapolate additional meaning from the first five commandments, as their subject matter is overtly religious and philosophical. These latter five commandments, however, can pose more of a challenge. Why? Simply because they're so clearly tied to human behaviors. They are explicit prohibitions on things people should not do. These commandments' literal definitions are so obvious that many people fail to even consider there might be additional layers of meaning. In reading these commandments, many people make the mistake of being so confident in their own sense of understanding that they fail to actually understand. But, as you will see, these last five commandments are absolutely just as complex as the five that preceded them.

To understand this sixth commandment, you may need to first overcome the sense of cliché, which may push you to dismiss the possibility of deeper meaning. Then, you should remember the premise: the Ten Commandments are the terms of Yahweh's marriage covenant with His bride. Thus, this is not just a law — it is a marriage vow. And if this commandment was (and is) an essential part of His marriage, then the underlying principle should be applied to your own marriage.

"Don't kill."

It's so simple. It's also unfathomable for most people. "Of course I won't kill anyone" is a common thought for decent people. Unfortunately, that thought also serves to dismiss this commandment. If one feels that this commandment has no bearing on his or her life, they may naturally lack the motivation to give it additional thought. The failure to understand the totality of this commandment sets one up to be oblivious to its violation. Or, at least, the violation of its underlying principle.

God told His bride not to murder. He didn't put any qualifiers with this instruction. He just said, "Don't." Therefore, this commandment should be interpreted broadly. Most people were raised to believe that this commandment simply means, "Don't murder other people." That is certainly is the literal meaning of this, but it isn't all of it.

Again, this commandment is part of a marriage covenant. More specifically, this was Yahweh's marriage covenant with humanity (through the Israelites). The only two parties in this covenant were God and Israel. If Israel was not supposed to kill, whom were they not supposed to kill? Obviously, one another. But also, God.

Humanity broke the sixth commandment at Calvary.

People killed the human life of God.

Sin broke the marriage covenant with Yahweh.

The bride killed her Spouse.

Quite literally, it was humanity that nailed Christ to a beam and tortured Him to the point of heart failure. At that point (and certainly at times before then), the Israelites broke their marriage covenant with God. The bride literally killed her Husband. If that had been the end, it would have signified the end of God's marriage to humanity. But it wasn't the end.

In the Gospel of John, Christ is quoted as saying that no one takes His life from Him. Instead, He says that He will give up His life. Reading the Gospel closely, one may notice that Christ didn't say that people couldn't take His life. He simply said that they can't take from Him the life that He has given away. He's not talking about the physical act of ending His human life. He is talking about the blame that goes along with murdering someone.

At Calvary, Christ died. People killed Him. But the blame didn't fall on the people.

Why?

In His death, Christ took the blame for all of humanity's sins. This included (and still includes) the sin of actually killing Him. As such, in God's eyes — and for that matter, in truth — no one killed Christ. Christ gave His own life.

Again, why?

God wants to be married to humanity. He wants Israel to be

able to be His spouse. He wants you. And He went through hell to make that happen.

The sacrifice of Christ made it so that humanity's sins never happened. It erased the guilt. Despite what one may see through humanity's flawed perspective of history, the Bride has truthfully never broken her vows. She didn't break the sixth commandment, nailing her Husband to a cross, because it never happened. Her marriage covenant is still valid and binding. It is a paradox, a beautiful riddle. It's the only thing that allows mankind a meaningful relationship with God.

Just because Christ covered the sin of breaking of the sixth commandment at Calvary, doesn't mean that husbands and wives are not capable of violating it again with their human spouses. Humanity's murder of Christ wasn't a premeditated act. There wasn't a universal, multi-generational, intentional conspiracy to cause the death of Christ. Nevertheless, that's what inadvertently happened. Then, isn't it possible that folks could also inadvertently "kill" their earthly spouses?

A door slammed.
An engine roared.
Gravel flew.
Sarah sat in the kitchen. In the dark. Furious.

The evening had started okay. She and Robert, her husband, had begun planning their annual summer vacation. About twenty minutes in, the conversation took a turn for the worse. Somewhere between "Martha's Vineyard" and "staycation," the mood became tense.

Sarah wanted a "real" vacation. Robert wanted to save money.

Both were resolute.

The proverbial excrement hit the turbine when Robert toxically expressed his opinion that Sarah might gain greater sense of frugality if she got a "real job." Robert then stupidly followed up this caustic advice with a lengthy monologue. He covered a range of topics but primarily focused on berating Sarah for lavish spending, unrealistic expectations, and "living like a spoiled brat."

Sarah didn't take it well.

Having long-held the belief that "the best defense in a good offense," Sarah attacked. She used all of the ammunition in her arsenal, went back to the armory, restocked, reloaded, and then went at him again with the focused determination of a Kamikaze pilot. She flew furiously through his history of reckless investments. She dove into the poor choices he had made prior to their marriage (to one of which he still owed alimony). And Sarah crashed in a firestorm upon Robert's shortcomings as a father and husband.

At that point, whether it was cowardice or wisdom, Robert left.

And there she sat. Alone. Enraged.

Robert sped. The only thing hotter than his temper was the cherry of his cigarette. Those rides were becoming too familiar. Robert had only two consolations: he had a carton of reds in the passenger seat, and the highway didn't seem to mind how loud he cussed.

A little more than two thousand years ago, Christ talked to a group of villagers about their hearts. He quoted the sixth commandment and then explained that murder was caused by anger. Anger, he said, made one as guilty as a murderer. It was a bold statement. In doing so, He (being God) essentially expanded the prohibition of the sixth commandment to include mere emotions. He amplified the understanding of what it meant to kill someone.

Christ got it. He understood that the Ten Commandments were a marriage covenant. And, as in all marriages, the conditions of emotions are as important as any physical deeds. Covenants aren't broken merely at the point of ultimate action. They are broken when the hearts of those involved are compromised. Love doesn't die only at divorce, it fades through the gradual degradation of a husband's and wife's emotions.

Yahweh's restriction against murder was a warning for His bride to guard her emotions. To maintain the covenant, His bride had to learn self-control. The same is true of all marriage covenants.

For a marriage to flourish, both spouses must learn to govern their emotions. Anger is toxic. It's a poison that kills covenants. Left unchecked, negative emotions lead to negative behaviors. And, since your spouse is your mirror, your spouse will reflect your propensity toward anger and your misguided behavior.

As with honor, the virtue of self-control must be realized universally. It cannot be relegated toward select people. A husband who is kind toward his wife, while hateful toward others, is a hateful husband. A wife who loves her husband but rages against her children is a hateful wife. A murderous heart cannot fully love. Murderers make lousy spouses. Angry spouses are no better.

The sixth commandment prohibits both the killing of the Spouse (God) as well as the murder of others. It exists with the understanding that how one treats those outside the covenant is equally important to how one treats those within the covenant. Likewise, your attitude toward people other than your spouse will reveal the true character of your heart, even if you seemingly regard your spouse with kindness.

Great marriages are the product of spouses who reject malice. They function in grace instead of anger. When conflicts arise, they lay down their lives, instead of rising to their own defense or blaming others. Just as Christ exhibited sacrificial love through the control He exerted on His own destiny, husbands and wives must also learn to exercise sacrificial self-control over their emotions and actions.

When the Apostle Paul wrote that husbands should love their wives in the same way that Christ loved the Church, he did so in the context of a larger discussion on the topic of how couples should relate toward one another. In that passage, Paul laid out an intricate riddle. He initially stated that wives should be subject to their husbands, just as the Church is subject to God. Many people stop there, but Paul didn't. He went on to state that husbands ought to demonstrate their love toward their wives by laying down their own desires. Husbands, Paul said, should be like Christ and lay down their lives. Obviously, Paul was not advocating for suicide. What he was getting at was something much more sacrificial: respect.

In many marriages, and particularly in troubled marriages, husbands and wives often fight as they each try to assert their wills over one another. These conflicts are common and manifested in a wide array of situations. For instance, many husbands and wives have disagreements with regard to how their lives should be lived. They may fight over where they should live, how they should raise their kids, what church they should attend, how their money should be spent, and many other matters. These conflicts often stem from a lack of respect. When a husband denies his wife's will in favor of his own, he is fundamentally showing disregard toward her. When a wife fights to assert her will over her husband's will, she is guilty of dishonoring her husband. This is exactly what Paul was addressing; the question of whose will should win.

Paul's answer was perfect. Instead of making a blanket ruling and picking one sex as having the ultimate prevailing will, Paul's solution was steeped in equity and equality. Paul said that, yes, a wife should submit her will to the will of her husband. He then also said that a husband should give up his own will for the good of his wife. Basically, Paul was saying, "Husband, you get to be in charge, but you cannot exert your own will, because your will is dead." So whose will prevails? No one's. Both parties must relinquish their own selfish desires. Husbands and wives must both focus their lives on respecting one another and seeking each other's good. Because, as Paul explained, the two are one. When they love and respect one another, they are showing love and respect toward their own selves.

Colin and Sue were at an impasse. Though they had only been married for six months, they had grown apart. Once their gloriously lustful honeymooning had stopped and their everyday living had begun, problems arose.

Colin began slowly drifting back into the lifestyle patterns that he has established as a bachelor. He rediscovered old friendships. Along with those friendships, he also rediscovered his appetite for bourbon. And it was a rapacious appetite.

Meanwhile, Sue began pursuing her own, less intoxicated, interests. She loved to travel, and so that's what she did. Every weekend, she was in another city, meeting new friends, seeing new sights, and generally feeling very cultured and cosmopolitan.

"This works for us," they both reasoned. Sue's times away from home provided Colin with the opportunity to indulge his proclivities without either one of them causing much disruption to the other. Initially, it seemed like a good arrangement; they each got to do as they pleased without interference. They were thrilled with how their little arrangement allowed them to have very little impact on one another.

Over time, however, their disparate lifestyles began to take a toll on their marriage. They couldn't identify what was wrong, but they both began to feel a growing sense of dissatisfaction within their marriage. Though technically still newlyweds, they didn't feel that their relationship was particularly romantic. The fire had gone out and the coals had cooled. But instead of hate, what they felt toward one another was something much more disconcerting: apathy. They didn't fight, because they had grown indifferent toward one another. The lack of emotion was the hardest to bear. The emotional void was a constant reminder that what they once had was gone. And they didn't know why.

Beyond harboring negative emotions, there is yet another layer to this commandment as it relates to marriage. It directly addresses what happened to Sue and Colin's marriage. For many husbands and wives, it should be among their foremost concerns.

A murder nullifies a person's life. Dead people have very little functional value. That's why they're buried in the ground. Even the corpse of a loved one is not something that sane people want to have laying around. While the memories and legacy of the life of the deceased can be very influential, the actual human remains provide very little positive impact.

When a spouse chooses to live as though their other half is non-existent, they functionally kill their spouse. Colin and Sue's marital discontent stemmed from the fact that they had negated one another's existence. While they were proud of the fact that they didn't impact one another, they failed to realize that their lack of impact on one another was the very thing that undermined their marriage. By living largely separate lives, they were essentially living as though they were each widowed. Even though they didn't feel hatred toward one another, they had killed the relational part of one another.

The sixth commandment's instruction to refrain from murder should serve as a warning to abstain from behaviors and attitudes that have the same functional effect as murder. As previously discussed, one shouldn't build an extra-marital relationship that functionally supersedes the exclusivity owed to their spouse (regardless of whether or not the third party is actually superseding their spouse). Likewise, husbands and wives should be careful to ensure that they are not functionally negating the lives of their respective spouses. If you live as though your spouse is dead, you are living as though you killed them. You are (probably without intention or awareness) violating the underlying principle of the sixth commandment: the preservation of life. Or, as it philosophically relates to marriage, the preservation of the impact of the life of your spouse on your own life.

Husbands' lives should be so intrinsically tied to those of their wives that their impact is constantly felt. Their existence should always have positive ramifications. The fact that they are alive should be absolutely consistently consequential in the daily lives of their wives. And the same is entirely true of wives toward their husbands — wives should remain fully alive within the day-to-day lives of their husbands.

In great marriages, both parties live as though the other is not dead. They do not kill one another. Taken literally, this is so obvious that it shouldn't even have to be said. Functionally, however, couples often forget these simple truths. Successful marriages require both parties to constantly consider their ramifications on one another. Their lives are consciously and perpetually entwined. They are inseparable. Furthermore, instead of negating their spouse's existence, a great husband or wife will actually strive to affirm and strengthen their partner's role in their life. They will actively seek opportunities for their spouse to impact their life.

In doing so, they underscore the honor of their covenant and the truth of their lives.

Chapter Seven
Thou shalt not commit adultery.

Given that this is a marriage covenant, the seventh commandment should be somewhat of a no-brainer. It speaks directly to the intimate acts of marriage. That is to say, it's about sex. Just as sexuality is the root of marriage, this commandment regarding sex is fundamental and reinforces the totality of the Ten Commandments.

In the minds of the ancient Israelites, the number seven was representative of completion. God completed the creation of the earth on the seventh day. There are seven primary musical notes that humans are able to hear. The Biblical year is constructed around seven festivals, the full cycle of which completes and then restarts the year. In the book of Revelation, the number seven appears many times. The Apostle John's spiritual visions feature seven churches, seven spirits, seven stars, seven seals, seven trumpets, and many other sevens. Through Revelation alone, one can see that the number seven represents the spiritual completeness, or totality, of heaven and Earth, Yahweh and His bride.

This seventh commandment represents the totality of God's marriage covenant. In it, Yahweh sums up the other commandments. The seventh commandment is the total commandment. Everything that mattered within the structure of God's marriage to His bride can be summed up in this commandment.

The first commandment was "You shall have no other gods before me." This commandment reflects the Father's desire to have an exclusive relationship. Adultery is the ultimate act of marital non-exclusivity. Having sex with someone other than one's own spouse clearly negates the exclusive nature of marriage. A marriage, wherein a third party comes before either of the spouses, is an adulterous marriage.

"Thou shalt not make unto thee any graven image." Yahweh refuses to allow Himself to be replaced by another. He doesn't want a surrogate. Adultery is fundamentally the act of surrogating the sexual role of one's spouse. A mistress is a replacement for a wife.

"Thou shalt not take the name of the Lord thy God in vain." The authority of one's spouse is circumvented by adultery. A cuckolded husband has no authority in his marriage. Adultery is an extreme violation of the responsibility and trust that should exist between married couples.

"Remember the Sabbath day to keep it holy." The Sabbath is an act of reconnection. In marriage, that reconnection is conveyed physically through sex. Obviously, sexual adultery is the most literal perversion of the marital Sabbath.

"Honor thy father and thy mother." Adultery dishonors both the betrayed spouse as well as the adulterer. It is the ultimate marital degradation. Adultery fundamentally dishonors the victimized spouse.

"Thou shalt not kill." The revelation of adultery generally produces feelings of anger and hatred, and it even occasionally leads to actual murder. In a higher sense, an adulterer also functionally "kills" their spouse by engaging in behavior that negates their existence. Or, at the very least, it negates their spouse's role.

"Thou shalt not commit adultery." Exactly.

"Thou shalt not steal." Adultery is theft. It is the act of taking something that is not one's belonging. Adultery involves both the theft of the perpetrating spouse and the theft of the marital relationship. This often results in the theft of the faithful spouse's emotions, time, sense of security, finances, children, and much more.

"Thou shalt not bear false witness against thy neighbor." One cannot commit adultery without lying. Even if an adulterer is forthcoming about their affair, he or she has essentially reduced their marriage covenant to a lie. An adulterous spouse has misrepresented their own self, their spouse, and their covenant. Through adultery they've also added the sin of perjury to their list of offenses.

"Thou shalt not covet." Coveting is rooted in the desire to obtain pleasure from something that doesn't belong to you. A person cannot engage in adultery without coveting.

Each of the Ten Commandments is tied to the seventh commandment. In the context of a marriage covenant, to break the seventh commandment is to break every commandment. The reason most marriages become casualties of adulterous affairs is because adultery violates the totality of what it truly means to be married. Even folks who deny the existence of God and the authority of the Ten Commandments almost universally feel that sexual infidelity is an unforgivable injustice within a marriage. It's often the irreparable hole in the dike. Once it's happened, it's just a matter of time before the marriage is under water.

Pam sat across a table from Will. Coffee spit through a machine and landed unceremoniously in a mug. No one reached for it.

The clock on the microwave showed the time: 5:17 a.m. For Pam this was too early. For Will, it was too late.

Will had been up all night texting his girlfriend, as teenagers are inclined to do. Only this time, instead of playful innuendos and dumb jokes, the correspondence was gut-wrenching.

"She's been seeing him for three months," Will lamented to his mother.

The room was silent for three minutes.

"What do you want?" asked Pam.

"What's impossible," answered Will with frustration in his voice. "I want it to have never happened. I want *her* to have never happened."

Pam was listening to her son, but her mind was elsewhere. She was remembering how she felt six years earlier, when she had discovered the billing statements from a credit card that she was unaware her husband had. As she read, she felt as though the world was grinding to a halt.

As it turned out, the dates of his recent "business trip to Detroit" corresponded with charges at a hotel in Virginia Beach. A few weeks later, when he was "called into a late meeting" and arrived home two hours late? On that night, he had spent ninety dollars at the Holiday Inn across from his office. There were recurring charges for cell phone service for an account she didn't recognize. He had also made purchases — large ones — at various retailers in the neighboring city.

After twelve years of marriage, she knew it was over.

Pam put the incriminating credit card statement under a rock on the front porch and went to the bank. There, she moved every dollar they had to a new account. Then, she cried.

Now, seated in front of her, Pam was watching her son experience the heartbreak of infidelity in his own small way. She knew the pain. It was a profound mixture of rage and emptiness.

"I just feel like everything is a lie," said Will, as Pam's thoughts rejoined the conversation.

"That's because — now — it is," Pam said with a voice that was affected with equal parts of contempt and sympathy.

Adultery makes everything a lie. A marriage is fundamentally an agreement of exclusivity. Adultery breaches that agreement. Therefore, the entire marriage covenant becomes a lie.

An adulterous husband is not a husband. A betrayed wife, no longer has an exclusive claim over her husband — effectively negating what it means for her to be a wife. Their agreement is broken. Everything becomes untrue.

Fortunately, the opposite is also true. A faithful husband is certainly a husband. He maintains his covenant. His wife is fully his wife. Their marriage is true.

To maintain a marriage, both spouses must remain faithful. In the best marriages, husbands and wives make no allowances for infidelity. They are vigilant to resist even the slightest temptations. They know how much is at stake.

Spouses in great marriages are proactive about remaining faithful. They consciously resist the inclination to build close relationships with members of the opposite sex to whom they are not married. And this applies to more than just physical relationships.

Many things contribute to affairs. Occasionally, they are the result of mere lust. At least as often, however, they result from other factors. A man may crave the adventure that he feels from an illicit lover. A woman may be drawn into adultery by the sense of companionship that she receives from another man. Compassion, respect, excitement, romance, interest, obligation, and many other factors can drive husbands and wives to seek gratification outside of their marriages.

Very few adulterers begin their affairs with the intention of committing adultery. When surveyed, most adulterers profess to have loved their spouses at the time of their adultery. Thus, it seems that the impetus for many affairs is not merely the intent to fill a deficit of love. More often, affairs are the result of the urge to satisfy subconscious needs and desires. The failure to identify weaknesses or threats is often what causes risky relationships to begin. And, once they begin, it can be very difficult to fend off the almost inevitable adultery.

Many (if not most) affairs are the result of one party seeking to satisfy a need in their own lives. These needs are generally more psychological than physiological. That is to say that they are mental and emotional needs — not merely physical urges. To categorize infidelity as merely a symptom of sexual appetite is to grossly underestimate the motivation behind such behavior.

A husband who is "addicted" to pornography is likely wrestling with much more than just an overwhelming libido. Perhaps what he actually desires is excitement. Maybe he's drawn to the fantasy of a being with a woman who truly enjoys sex, and he finds the feigned activities of porn stars to be an outlet through which he can vicariously experience such desire. Or, maybe a broken self-esteem causes him to actually crave the feelings of shame that he experiences after consuming such material.

What if a wife seeks flirtatious friendships with other men because she doesn't feel desired by her husband? What if her motivation is simply the reward of having a man openly value her contribution to his life? Is it possible that she opens herself up to such relationships because these other men offer her the security of having a "Plan B" in case her marriage ultimately does fail?

Such examples don't necessarily involve complete adultery in the most literal, copulatory sense of the word. They do, however, underscore the complexity of the factors that can open the door to adulterous behavior. It's important to look beyond the physical acts of sexual adultery and examine the underlying causes of such behavior. Often, the incentive is much more than a mere orgasm.

In the Bible, King David committed adultery with Bathsheba after seeing her bathing on her rooftop terrace. Why? Her beauty piqued his interest, but it was likely something else that caused him to actually follow through with the affair. His affair was not a spontaneous event, so it probably wasn't simply because he was aroused by the sight of her. He had plenty of wives and concubines through whom he could have satisfied any voyeuristic tendencies that he may have had. Considering that he was the king, he probably even had numerous wives that were at least as physically beautiful as Bathsheba. Perhaps his motivation was something deeper. Perhaps it was the fact that she was married to someone else. (She was "forbidden fruit.") Maybe it was just greed, the desire to have simply for the sake of having. Or maybe it was an attempt to overcome feelings of inferiority by exerting ultimate control over another man and his wife. (For those unfamiliar with this story, David ultimately forced Bathsheba's husband into a wartime suicide mission.) Whatever the cause, David's adultery was the result of a weakness that he failed to adequately manage.

Learning to identify weaknesses is a key step toward safeguarding yourself from infidelity. Be honest with yourself and with your spouse. Within your marriage, do you feel loved? Respected? Appreciated? Sexy? Successful? Honored? Excited? Peaceful? Secure? Satisfied? Craved? Accomplished? (Something else?) If the answer to these questions is anything less than a confident "Yes," you have a vulnerability that could compromise the integrity of your marriage.

If you've identified weaknesses in your own life, discuss them with your spouse. Be honest about your needs and feelings. Granted, you must do so in a way that is not accusatory. Remember, these are your weaknesses — not their shortcomings. Then, ask your spouse to help you overcome your vulnerabilities.

As you become increasingly aware of your own weaknesses, you will begin to more quickly identify potential threats. Then, you can develop ways to avoid or overcome such threats. This, in turn, produces strength.

Pray for the wisdom to view yourself objectively. Strive to have the sort of honesty in your marriage that allows the free and non-judgmental discussion of weaknesses. If adultery makes everything a lie, then perhaps truth is the antidote.

Be true.

Stay faithful.

Chapter Eight
Thou shalt not steal.

"Don't steal." That was Yahweh's instruction at Mount Sinai. Simple. Straight to the point. No qualifiers, conditions, nor exceptions. He just said, "Don't steal."

Yahweh didn't limit this commandment by adding qualifying statements. For instance, He didn't say, "Don't steal money from Me" nor "Don't steal from My temple" nor "Don't steal from your neighbors." Such additions would have actually reduced the scope of this command. He didn't include them. As such, this commandment is comprehensive; it covers every kind of theft. On this matter He neither beat around the bush nor minced words. To His bride, He was clear: "You, do not steal."

This marital agreement to refrain from theft comes across as somewhat unusual when compared to modern marriage vows. Today, typical Christian and Jewish weddings include vows related to fidelity, love, commitment, and other ideals, but they generally don't touch upon the subject of theft. While theft can certainly be inferred through vows that cover spousal duty, theft generally isn't mentioned directly. And it certainly is neither elevated nor emphasized as a stand-alone vow within modern marriage covenants.

Perhaps something has been missed.
Something important.

Tyson sat alone on a bench outside a downtown library. Or, at least, he was as alone as one can be in city of four million people. Anxiously, he checked his watch. Nine seconds later, he checked it again. Then, he checked it again.

Time passed. Slowly.

"Ty!"

A woman's gleeful voice shattered Tyson's compulsive interest in his watch. The voice belonged to Lori, his wife.

In a single motion, Tyson was on his feet and headed in the direction of the voice. Two steps later, the crowd broke, and he spotted Lori walking briskly toward him with a wide smile.

They embraced. It was romantic. And mushy.

"How'd it go?" asked Tyson, after a moment's pause.

"It's going to happen!" exclaimed Lori. "They've accepted my proposal, and we'll get to start this summer!"

Enthusiastically, Tyson embraced his wife.

"Congratulations, honey," said Tyson. "It's been a long time coming. I'm so glad this is happening for you."

"Thank you. For all of this," replied Lori as the glitter of tears began to shine from her eyes.

Lori just wrapped up a meeting with the city library's Board of Directors. The Board had assembled to review a proposal Lori submitted to revamp the library's longstanding art program for school children. During the meeting, the Board approved the proposal and, in doing so, brought one of Lori's lifelong ambitions within her reach. After years of pining, planning, preparing, her dream was finally becoming a reality.

Tyson and Lori hadn't always been as happy as they were on that day. Though they had been married for sixteen years, the first dozen or so were filled with the highs and lows that are common in most modern marriages. They had loved and fought and healed and festered. For much of their marriage, they had simply endured. But, about four years prior to their embrace outside the library, they realized something that set them on a new path toward enduring marital happiness. It was the thing which made that day possible; their marriage needed to be focused on giving instead of taking.

That simple realization transformed their marriage.

Prior, they had spent the first twelve years of their marriage preoccupied with their own individual wants. Tyson had felt that his happiness would come through the things that he could get from Lori: sex, children, gifts, and even the seemingly mundane household chores that she performed for the benefit of their family. Likewise, Lori had been focused on the fleeting joy that came through the money, security, and companionship that Tyson provided. When they appreciated their marriage, it was often closely associated with what they'd taken from the other person. Their marriage had been more about looting than giving. They had been takers. Thieves. And what they had stolen came from the other.

When Tyson and Lori shifted their perspective from "What can I get?" to "What can I give?" everything changed. For the first time, they saw that their actions had been adversarial toward one another. They had been living as though their happiness stood on the other side what they could get from one another. Yet, no matter how much they took, they always found reasons to want more. Fortunately, those days were over. Together, they made the commitment to seek each other's happiness. Their love became sacrificial. And the more they sacrificed, the more they received.

For years, Tyson approached sex as a way to satisfy his own desires. This bred insecurities in Lori, as she was casually objectified and often felt degraded as nothing more than a means to an end. However, when Tyson committed to seeking Lori's happiness instead of his own gratification, he discovered that physical pleasure wasn't the highest result of sexuality. Tyson came to realize that by giving his sexuality to Lori (instead of taking her sexuality for his own indulgence), he received intimacy and affection unlike anything he'd known before. By giving his body to her and seeking her happiness, he in turn experienced a much more gratifying sex life. Why? Because she gave back, focusing on his pleasure instead of her own insecurities. Together, they both became more unified in the moments when they were physically united.

In the same way, Lori had spent years resenting Tyson for their modest home. She had subconsciously resented him for not making enough resources available for her to get the type of house that she wanted in the location that she desired. When Lori became aware of her subconscious desire to take more from Tyson, she made the choice to alter her perspective. Instead of craving more and seeing Tyson's financial contributions as merely her own private trove to loot, she chose to focus on giving Tyson the security that he desired. In doing so, she harnessed her expectations and actions. Over time, Tyson grew to trust his wife's financial decisions. This resulted in an increased sense of security, which eventually led to Tyson feeling, for the first time in their marriage, they had the ability to make a new investment in a larger home.

Lori's success at the library was another result of their marital shift. For years, she wanted to create a more meaningful arts program for the children of her community. Tyson, however, had opposed her dream. He once felt that her time and resources would be better spent doing things for him and their family, exclusively. With time, Tyson came to see that his role as Lori's husband was incompatible with his selfish desire to be the thief of her life and dreams. Instead of taking, he chose to give. And by giving, they both found happiness.

Theft can take many forms, especially within marriages. Many spouses routinely steal joy, hope, and aspirations from their significant others. And certainly, people also steal material things and opportunities. In marriages, theft is particularly problematic, because the thievery of one party is reflected negatively in the life of their spouse. While theft does not necessarily beget theft, it does impact the emotional outlook of the victim. This can cause a wide array of ramifications that are less than beneficial, including insecurity, defensiveness, and bitterness. Regardless of the form, the act of stealing always leaves the victim with less than what they had before.

In marriages, perhaps the worst theft occurs when a spouse steals the most valuable resource in the world: another person's time. The minutes of one's human life are absolutely finite. Laborers trade those minutes to their employers for compensation. (Money is, in fact, just a tool by which people trade the hours of human effort and ability.) Parents give their lives' minutes to their children. Married folks often invest them with their spouses or their churches or with God. When a husband or wife misuses their spouse's time, they are stealing. This theft of one's time can happen either directly or indirectly. It is the latter when a husband or wife abuses the things that their spouse has traded or invested their time to gain. This can include money, children, relationships, hobbies, ministries, etc. If a wife harms her husband's relationship with his children, she has stolen from her husband. If a husband wastes his wife's money, he has stolen from his wife. There's a reason why "money issues" are a top cause of divorce, and it's not because of the money. It's because the misuse of the money earned by someone else is actually the theft of that other person's life. Whether financial or otherwise, theft can be disastrous. It often creates irreparable damage in marriages.

Spouses should approach their marriage with the understanding that it — the marriage — is their opportunity to give. It should never be seen as an opportunity to take. Marriages should be centered on giving.

By entering into a marriage covenant, a husband and wife should view their union as a partnership through which they can build something greater than what they could achieve on their own. When one spouse routinely steals from their other half, their mutual value is reduced. But, when both parties are committed to investing their lives together in a cycle of continual giving, the sum of their partnership increases in value. Consider a two very simple examples of this phenomenon:

A man and a woman each have one hundred coins. If the man takes the woman's coins, he then has two hundred and she has none. If he then spends fifty of the coins, he will have only one hundred and fifty coins. If the woman then does the same process, stealing one hundred coins and spending fifty, she is left with only one hundred coins. And, ultimately, between both of them, they've halved their collective wealth.

Now consider if the scenario had been focused on giving and creating value, instead of taking and using. Suppose the man gave his one hundred coins to the woman, leaving him with none. Knowing that he shouldn't take from her, he instead goes out and earns one hundred more. Together, they would then have three hundred coins. If she then reciprocated by giving and earning to replenish her purse, their wealth would again increase. And it could continue endlessly.

These are oversimple examples, but they demonstrate truths: theft reduces the whole, and there is a better way to find personal growth. And this extends beyond money. When a husband steals and wastes his wife's time, they are collectively left with less time. However, when a wife gives her husband support in his career, they both reap the benefits. In marriage, one cannot take from his or her spouse without taking from the sum of their union. Theft always does at least one of two things: it reduces the whole and/or it reduces the opportunity to increase the whole.

"She makes me miserable." This feeling is often one of the foremost complaints among husbands in failing marriages. It's worded in a vast number of ways, but the sentiment is usually the same. And it's revealing. Such thoughts show that those husbands' true, overarching motivation is to take happiness from their spouse. When the largest grievance is centered on what someone is not getting, it shows that the grieved is focused on taking — not giving.

When people marry because "he makes me happy" or "she makes my life easier," they've got it all wrong. Every engaged couple should hear this truth: you shouldn't get married so that you can be happier or have your life improve. You should get married so that you can improve your spouse's life. Your marriage should be for them. Your life should be absorbed by a steadfast obsession with giving your life to your spouse.

In an ideal world, everyone would enter a marriage with the eager desire to benefit his or her spouse. Feelings of success and fulfillment would come from seeing the other person's life improve. And all would feel that marriage is worth having, even when it does nothing to improve one's own lot in life.

Selflessness is the key. Denying one's own interests unlocks limitless potential within your spouse. When both spouses are preoccupied with stealing one another's lives, they eventually find that they are both completely drained. Fortunately, the opposite is also true: when both spouses are fully committed to investing their lives for the good of one another, they soon find that their sum greatly exceeds the total of their individual contributions.

People — men especially — often proudly make grandiose statements about how they would be willing to die for their loved ones. And, sure, given the heroic opportunity, they might actually jump in front of a train or take bullet to save their spouse. That's cool. It's a huge, albeit highly unlikely, act of giving. However, instead of dying for one's spouse, a far greater challenge and reward is often found in the act of living for one's spouse. And it's something that one can actually plan and act upon.

Forget dying for your spouse. Live for your spouse. Completely. Lay down your life. Let it go. And then fully commit your life to the service and devotion of your spouse. Support your spouse's dreams. Fulfill their hopes. Provide them with more abilities and opportunities than they could have garnered on their own. Through the act of giving your life to your spouse, you reject an inclination toward theft and discover transformative value in your marriage.

Chapter Nine
Thou shalt not bear false witness against thy neighbor.

The ninth commandment is generally understood to be a prohibition against lying. Certainly, that is the simplest understanding of this vow. And it is accurate. That should not be dismissed. Truth is fundamental to the health of any relationship. In the context of a marriage, it is vital. Nevertheless, as with each of the Ten Commandments, there are more layers and deeper meaning within this vow.

English translations of this commandment make it seem as though Yahweh was simply telling His bride to not lie about other people. That is absolutely part of the commandment, but it misses some of the meaning. In Hebrew, the word that is read as "neighbor" actually has a much broader meaning. It is the word *rea*. Rea is translated throughout the Old Testament using a wide range of English words and phrases. It often appears simply as "another." Frequently, it takes the form of "friend." Instead of "neighbor," the most literal English translation of this word is actually closest to the word "companion." Your rea is your companion. As such, this commandment doesn't just pertain to a person who lives next door. It actually speaks foremost to one's companion.

And this was a marriage vow.

Essentially, this ninth vow declares that Yahweh's bride is to refrain from bearing false witness against her companion. Obviously, within the context of a marriage, one's preeminent companion is one's spouse. Yahweh was Israel's marital Companion. And Israel was supposed to honor her Companion by being truthful.

"Bear false witness" is also interesting. It's easy to gloss over it and miss some of its full meaning. The word translated as "bear" is actually a Hebrew word meaning "to respond." It's not just talking about something one carries, like a burden or a duty. No, it's actually less about being proactive and more about reactivity. It's something that follows something else. It's a response.

"False witness." It's a simple concept: when testifying as a witness, don't say something that is false. Sounds easy enough, especially if you never intend on being subpoenaed. However, things take on a new meaning when you consider that the first chapter of the book of Acts has a quote from Christ stating that the Church "shall be my witnesses." Elsewhere in Scripture, this idea is reinforced; the Church — His bride — is to be His witness throughout the earth. His bride is instructed to be a light to the world, to testify of the goodness of God, and be an example of His righteousness.

When you connect the dots between these ideas, "Thou shalt not bear false witness against your neighbor" begins to take on a new meaning. It becomes, "As you respond to life, don't be false as a witness of your Companion." And again, the "Companion" is Yahweh.

The ninth commandment was the bride's vow to be truthful both toward and concerning her Groom. Yahweh knew His people would be tested; they would endure hatred, war, crime, rape, and all of the sins of the fallen world. He also knew His bride would experience blessings, such as wealth, love, success, sex, children, mercy, and everything else that makes humanity beautiful. Through all of this, Yahweh wanted His bride to respond in a way that was consistently true to who He was in her life. Come what may.

Earthly marriages should have that same commitment.

Truth is central to trust. It's the fuel that enables relationships to move forward. Without truth, marriages fail.

Take a moment to think about a couple you know that has a strong marriage. Among their many positive attributes, it is almost guaranteed that you perceive both the husband and wife as being consistently honest with one another. And they probably are. Conversely, if you think about a couple with a poor marriage, you likely also know that they lie to one another. It's interesting that almost everyone, regardless of their background, associates honest spouses with good marriages and lying spouses with bad marriages. It's subconsciously recognized because it is true and universal.

Marriages need truth.

The sort of truth marriages require certainly includes what one spouse says to another. And it goes further. It is directly part of many of the other commandments. A wife who denies her role as a wife is lying to her husband. A husband who publicly castigates his wife is falsely representing who she is in his life: the reflection and other half of him. It's all connected.

Esther has a problem: her husband, Charles, is lazy. Throughout his adult life, Charles has never been able to hold down a job.

He has had many, but they have never lasted long. His half-hearted attempts to withstand a simple forty-hour workweek and the unrelenting urge to repeatedly finger his alarm clock's snooze button always combine to make him an essentially useless employee. So he is fired. Often. And when he isn't fired, it is only because he beats his employers to the punch by simply quitting without notice. Naturally, this severe character flaw is a cancer within his marriage.

Charles' professional problems are the result of many sins. Yes, a significant factor is sloth, which society even once considered to be one of the "seven deadly sins" (back when society actually believed in sin). Also at play is a lack of self-control, a chronic inclination toward lying, and many other vices. All of this has resulted in a résumé that scares off all but the most desperate or careless of employers.

Aside from the financial burden that Charles places on his family, his actions have taken a much deeper toll on his marriage. Esther understands that Charles lacks maturity. To her credit, she chooses to love him despite knowing that. That part, she has forgiven. The part that she has not been able to dismiss is Charles' unholy rejection of his role as her husband.

A husband — even an immature husband — has an obligation to strive to provide for his family. Charles doesn't even try. This is not a small flaw. Being a provider is fundamental to who a husband is — or should be — within his marriage. It's such an important topic that the Apostle Paul sent a letter to Timothy explaining that a man who doesn't provide for his family "has denied the faith and is worse than an unbeliever." That's about as serious as it gets.

By denying his role as a provider, Charles bears false witness against Esther. Charles is lying to Esther when he tells her that he will serve as her husband but then fails to provide for her. And there's more. As her husband, Charles is Esther's witness to those he encounters. Charles represents Esther and vice versa. When

Charles lies to his employers (telling them he will perform a job and then failing to do so), he is falsely representing Esther, whether or not the employers realize it on a conscious level. Inherently, Esther's reputation, and the reputation of their family are harmed by the image Charles' projects. Sadly, it's guilt by association.

Many books have been sold that talk about the value of respect within marriage. Most of those books state that respect is a primary desire of men. That's true, but it's also shortsighted. Respect is also a primary desire of women. (It is impossible to demonstrate love without respect, and virtually everyone acknowledges that women desire to be loved.)

In any interpersonal relationship, levels of respect for one another are often how one is able to gauge another's affection toward him or her. For instance, if a family member were to publicly denounce you as an idiot, you would likely (and probably accurately) conclude that your family member doesn't have a high level of affection for you. Fortunately, the opposite is also true. Public praise reinforces your perception of the praiser's affection toward you. If someone stands on a stage and sincerely says that you're wonderful and smart and kind and necessary, you're likely going to walk away feeling as though the speaker admires you.

Why?

Why is it that something as simple as public praise can have a profound effect, not just on your self-esteem, but also on your perception of the speaker's feelings toward you? After all, it's just a string of words. And people can lie.

The answer lies in this ninth commandment.

When someone publicly praises you, you value their words because they are providing a witness (or testimony) to your goodness. Not only are they respecting you, they are also proselytizing others to believe in your goodness. While a private compliment may feel nice, public praise goes further and deeper because it bears witness to whom you are. A private compliment whispers, "I respect you," but public praise screams to the world, "This person is worthy of respect!" A strong witness goes a long way.

How you project your respect for your spouse can have a tremendous impact on your spouse's belief in your affection toward them. You are their most credible spokesperson. By living as a true witness to the higher qualities of your spouse, you are able to build their reputation among others while shoring up their confidence in your affection.

The degree to which you serve as a positive or negative witness of your spouse directly correlates to their sense of being loved and respected. A silent witness is a negative witness. Society is suspicious, and silence is viewed as consent. Think about it.

If a wife refuses to wear her wedding band when she is in public with her husband, she is a false witness to the marital status and morality of her husband. Doing so gives the appearance that she is an unmarried woman in the company of a married man. If their interactions are even remotely flirtatious or affectionate, it gives the appearance that her husband is engaged in an adulterous relationship. Likewise, if a husband refuses to list his marital status on his social media profiles, he is a false witness against his wife. If a wife never praises her husband publicly, those in their social circles (including her husband) will naturally begin to suspect that either the husband is not praiseworthy or the wife has lost her respect and affection for her husband.

Imagine that you have a coworker named Bob. Bob is generally a nice guy, and he is married to Sue. If, over the course of a few years, Bob never says anything positive about Sue, it's unlikely that you will assume that Sue is a person with great qualities.

Conversely, if Bob always says great things about Sue, you will likely be convinced that Sue is a pretty great person and that Bob loves her. And Sue would probably also feel confident that Bob loves and respects her.

This happens all the time. Everyone experiences it and knows it's true — even if he or she has never consciously thought about it before. Others judge one spouse's character based on the other spouse's testimony.

Now, think about how damaging one can be when one goes beyond merely being silent and regresses to actively defaming his or her spouse. Unfortunately, spouses often fall on this side of the spectrum. They say derisive, disrespectful things about their spouses: "The old ball and chain." "He let himself go." "She's a terrible driver." "He's like a bull in a china shop." "He's an immature jerk." "She's a frigid [w]itch." And we've all heard much worse. Such defamatory words (and the attitudes that go along with them) kill marriages. They are poison. They breed insecurities and anger. And they're a false witness.

An honest husband who truly understands the value and role of his wife is incapable making a derisive comment about her. It would be too painful for him. He knows that the "flaws" that he sees in her are merely his perception of his own reflection. To defame her is to defame himself, which brings them both down. And he recognizes that she deserves the highest pedestal. Why? Because she is his Good.

In all of this, remember that the commandment given by Yahweh to His bride was specifically reactive. As previously explained, the "bear" in "shalt not bear false witness" is a response. This is important. Many feel that being an occasional, proactive, positive witness toward their spouse is sufficient to ensure their spouse's knowledge of their affection. It's not. Occasional, grand statements of praise, while certainly beneficial, are not enough.

True, lasting happiness isn't developed in occasional moments. True happiness comes through an unrelenting stream of small, positive moments. For instance, if an employee's job is generally miserable but punctuated annually by a sizable bonus or positive review, the employee will still not be fully engaged. Nor will that employee find happiness in her work. Rather, the employee would be better served by having bosses who sought to make her day-to-day experience positive, instead of merely attempting to make amends through lone, grand gestures. That may seem somewhat counterintuitive, but it's true. Let's bring this concept home...

Many parents make the mistake of thinking they can assure their children of their affection through irregular, large gestures. They buy their sixteen-year-olds new cars. They take their sons camping. They go on summer vacations to Disney World. They even buy into the myth of "quality time," which is supposedly a magical moment wherein families can bond during a finite, pre-scheduled period of time. Then, the parents wonder why their kids are distant and rebellious. ("Why don't you love me?! Can't you see how much money I spent on you?!")

Affection cannot be effectively communicated when it's demonstrated only through proactive gestures.

Why?

The vast majority of life's experiences are reactive. Every day, people react to their environments and experiences. They go to work. They receive questions from their kids. They get stuck in traffic. They get hurt. They talk to friends and colleagues. They experience blessings. If a person's affection for his or her spouse isn't evident in all of those reactive moments, their spouse is unlikely to be satisfied by the rare moments of proactivity. It is how one reacts to life that shows their true character, values, and commitments. This is why it's important to be a true witness to one's spouse when reacting to every moment of everyday life. Your reactions will do more to improve your life than anything you could ever hope to do proactively. Reactions are where the rubber hits the road. Even praise is a reaction to the goodness, accomplishments, and virtues of another.

Yahweh wanted His bride's reactions to be a positive witness to His goodness throughout their daily experiences. The Israelites vowed they would do just that. Shouldn't you do the same for your spouse?

Chapter Ten
Thou shalt not covet.

Covetousness sums up the fundamental problem in many marriages. People misdirect their lust. They so badly want the wrong things that they then live life badly. Instead of focusing their desire on the pleasure of their spouse, their home, and other healthy ends, they become obsessed with targets that are beyond their reach (or, at least, should be beyond their reach). This is the vice the tenth commandment addresses.

Yahweh's prohibition against covetousness was the last item in His marriage vows. Whether it's Moses' final conversation with God, King David's deathbed conversation with Solomon, Christ's last words during His ascension, or the closing chapter of the book of Revelation, the Bible clearly places a strong value on final statements. Often, they encapsulate the essence of everything that had been previously said. They are the summation of the spirit of the message. In the same way, the Israelite's tenth vow to Yahweh speaks directly to the heart of what it would require to successfully keep the marriage of the divine and humanity.

The terms of the tenth commandment are surprisingly detailed, especially when compared to many of the preceding commandments. In the vow, Yahweh states, "You shall not covet your neighbor's wife, and you shall not desire your neighbor's house, his field or his male servant or his female servant, his ox or his donkey or anything that belongs to your neighbor." At first glance, this seems to be an oddly specific list of dissimilar things: a wife, a house, a male servant, a female servant, an ox, a donkey, or "anything."

Huh?

Semantically, the "anything" certainly could have covered all of the other items in the list. So was Yahweh simply being redundant? Why would He list a bunch of very specific things and then throw in a blanket statement that essentially covers everything?

There are only two logical options to consider: either God was a poor writer or there was a specific purpose to the way He worded the tenth commandment. Most believers likely agree that the latter option is true; Yahweh deliberately chose every word for a specific purpose.

But what purpose? What could it possibly mean?

The depth of Scripture knows no bounds. Things that mean certain things can often also mean many other things, but that doesn't make the original meaning any less true. The Bible is filled with riddles and metaphors and clues and allusions. It's very rare that any particular verse in the Bible has only a singular meaning regarding only a singular topic or situation without any discernible bearing on any other ideas or situations.

This entire book is predicated on the idea that the Ten Commandments were so much more than just a list of ten laws. As explained since the first chapter, the Ten Commandments were also a marriage contract between Yahweh and the Israelites. And, taken a step further, those same commandments were also an outline for how human marriages ought to be governed. And the Ten Commandments are absolutely much more than even that. Nevertheless, none of those diverse layers of meaning undermine the face value of the plain text of the Ten Commandments. This book, like any other exercise in Biblical exegesis, shouldn't be viewed as a way to get to "the true" meaning. That implies that the face value is somehow not equally true. Instead, this should be considered simply a deeper understanding of the fuller meaning of this part of the Bible.

So, look deeper.

The first clue that this commandment holds a deeper meaning is found in the only explicit marital specification. Yahweh says that the Israelites should not covet their "neighbor's wife." The Hebrew word used for "wife" is *ishet*, which means the wife of someone. This is different from the Hebrew words used for "spouse" and "husband." When the tenth commandment says "wife" it means wife. Which leads to some questions: Why did Yahweh specifically underscore the prohibition against coveting someone else's wife? Isn't it also forbidden to covet someone's husband? Certainly, coveting a husband is also forbidden by the "and anything" clause. So why would Yahweh emphasize coveting a neighbor's wife and not also emphasize coveting a neighbor's husband?

Why?

The reason is simple: Yahweh has a wife. He does not have a husband.

As covered earlier, the word for "neighbor" essentially means one's companion. And in a marriage, one's principal companion is one's spouse. Yahweh was the most immediate Companion of the Israelites. Thus, Yahweh was the husband of the wife the Israelites were forbidden from coveting. Moreover, as God's bride, Israel was forbidden from coveting both their own selves and the larger body of believers. At first blush, this may seem a little too abstract and circular to be clearly understood. You may ask, "How could the Israelites covet themselves?" The answer is simple: the same way people do today.

The word "covet" is largely misunderstood. This is probably because modern society ferociously promotes covetousness. And most people don't even realize it. Modern folks generally believe that "coveting" simply means "wanting something that isn't yours." That's an oversimplification. In the Hebrew text of this commandment, the word for "covet" is *chamad*. This word's most literal translation is "to take pleasure in." So while it is certainly inappropriate to simply want someone else's stuff, it is even more problematic to use someone else's property for your own selfish pleasure, particularly when it comes at the expense of the other person's pleasure.

A good example of this is found in the coveting of someone else's money. Simply desiring it may be problematic, but it may also motivate you to simply earn it, which is good. Getting pleasure from someone else's money, however, involves outright sin. This is because the only way to receive actual pleasure from someone else's money is to steal it from them. (If they had given or exchanged it to you, it would no longer be "someone else's" money — it would be *your* money.)

With this understanding, one can begin to comprehend the weight of Yahweh's prohibition against His bride coveting herself. The Israelites were being told to refrain from taking pleasure in their own selves. They were supposed to reject the notion that their own collective lives and accomplishments should be their goal and the source of their utmost pleasure. Their true pleasure should not be sought within themselves.

Throughout history, people have rejected this commandment and elevated their own lives and the collective life of humanity to an unholy level. It manifests itself in many ways. Hedonism is the idea that one's own pleasure should be one's moral compass. (Essentially, "if it feels good, do it.") Humanism is the belief that human intellect alone, exercised through rational thought, leads to the highest levels of human potential. Though these philosophies vary greatly, they share the same premise: true pleasure (joy, happiness, self-worth, etc.) should be found in one's own self. While a self-centered worldview may cause someone to feel pleasure, it has a couple of major flaws.

The first problem with self-covetousness (the pursuit of finding one's own pleasure through oneself) is that it denies the reality that true, lasting pleasure comes from God. The second problem is that it misdirects the focus of one's ambitions from another (God, a spouse, or even a literal neighbor) onto oneself. Self-centeredness is toxic to any relationship. It is inherently idolatrous, violating the first and second commandments. It ultimately does not produce happiness. It breeds a hunger that cannot be satisfied. All of this is toxic to any marriage, including both Yahweh's with Israel and any human union. Anyone who enters a marriage to seek their own pleasure is destined for hardship and disappointment. Fortunately, the opposite is also true. Spouses who live for the pleasure of their own husband or wife experience prosperous marriages.

The commandment also prohibits coveting someone else's house. From an Israelite perspective, Yahweh's "house" held multiple meanings. It included the Tabernacle, the physical home of God's presence on Earth and the sign of His sovereignty. It also meant someone's household, which is essentially the totality of their domain. Yahweh didn't want His bride to try to use His dominion for her own pleasure.

Coveting a "neighbor's field" was also disallowed. In the agricultural society of the ancient Israelites, a field was quite literally the realm of one's work. A field was the place wherein someone could exercise his or her productivity. It is tied directly to one's dominion. This clause, coupled with the previous one regarding one's house, instructed the Israelites to refrain from desiring to use God's dominion for their own selfish goals.

The fourth and fifth specifications pertain to male and female servants. The fact that Yahweh identified both sexes is curious, especially as it follows the gender-centric ban on coveting someone else's wife. From the most basic perspective, this seems to be inconsistent. However, with the understanding that the "wife" is actually referring to Yahweh's bride, this begins to make sense. God has only one wife (and no husband), but He also has servants who are both male and female. While the "Bride of Christ" is the collective body of believers, that bride is in turn comprised of servants who are both men and women. Those men and women represented the agency through which God would operate. By explicitly mentioning both male and female servants, Yahweh ensured that every individual who serves Him is protected from being misused by His bride for her own selfish pleasure. Just as people should not misuse the collective body (God's wife) for their own pleasure, they also shouldn't view individuals as a means to achieving their own selfish ambitions.

The tenth commandment also includes a restriction on coveting another's ox or donkey. To modern minds, this may seem like an arbitrary selection of animals. But God is not arbitrary. Oxen and donkeys are often referenced together throughout the Bible. Similar to how the bald eagle is considered by Americans to be symbolic of freedom and independence, those animals held deep meaning in ancient society. In the ancient Hebrew mind, oxen and donkeys bore significant connotations. First, they were both beasts of burden. Their primary value was their ability to get things done. They were the tractor-trailers of the ancient world, the mechanisms through which progress moved. Scripture places a high symbolic value on these particular animals.

Oxen were required for Temple services, both in the manual labor as well as the sacrificial ceremonies. They were often regarded as a metaphor for consecrated strength, a symbol through which the Israelites identified as a nation. Donkeys, on the other hand, were "unclean" and represented wild strength. From ancient times to this day, Jewish literature often associates donkeys with Gentile cultures (functionally, those who might be described as "non-believers"), due to their utilitarian importance despite their lack of constraint. Often, in both ancient and contemporary Jewish writings, the metaphor of a donkey is used to explain how "unclean" people can be used by God to advance the work of His kingdom. Together, the mentioned ox and donkey represented the mechanisms through which God advances His will on earth. That is to say that they represented utility.

In telling His bride to not covet her Companion's ox and donkey, Yahweh was instructing His bride to not covet the strength through which He would advance His kingdom. While the house and field represented *where* and the male and female servants represented *who*, the ox and donkey represented *how* Yahweh's power would be exercised. Essentially, Yahweh was telling His bride that under His dominion He would use His servants in both holy and secular mechanisms to advance His will.

It all comes down to power. Dominion, agency, and strength are all fundamental components of power. The restriction against coveting the Companion's house and land, male and female servants, and oxen and donkeys were essentially prohibitions against His bride using Yahweh's power for her self-serving pleasure.

Judy married well. Her husband, Gene, was a good man. Throughout the course of their lives together, Gene worked diligently to provide for his family. And, over the years, he forged a successful career that allowed them to live quite comfortably. Through Gene's power, their entire family was blessed.

Over the years, however, Judy became increasingly dissatisfied. Though she had everything she needed and most of what she wanted, Judy perpetually found herself craving just a little more. Her appetite for material goods started modestly, but it eventually grew to become insatiable. No matter what she procured or how high their income climbed, she was always craving something that was just beyond their financial reach.

As the years wore on and Judy's lustful materialism increased, she began to despise Gene. Whenever they couldn't afford her next impulse, she blamed the source of her buying power, her husband. She mercilessly attacked and berated him, insulting his abilities, wisdom, and effort. She faulted him for "not providing for their family," despite the fact that he alone, as the sole breadwinner, brought in an annual income was many times that of the median American household. Their marriage suffered traumatically.

Covetousness was the source of Judy's problem. And it affected her on every level outlined in the tenth commandment. Judy coveted her husband's wife, herself. She made her own pleasure her highest pursuit. By desiring to use Gene's dominion, agency, and strength (his career, work ethic, and effort, respectively) as her personal fount of everlasting pleasure, she drained the very well from which she had been sustained. And that well was her marriage.

The final component of the tenth commandment is the catch-all, "or anything," clause. Preceding that last clause are seven specific clauses. As explained in chapter seven, the number seven represents totality and completeness. The "or anything" statement underscores that completeness. As Yahweh's bride, the Israelites vowed to not covet anything that pertained to Yahweh. That promise to abstain from covetousness was the final component that sealed their marriage. As such, it's no surprise that it is also the very thing that makes or breaks many human marriages.

Elevating one's own pleasure above the wellbeing of one's spouse is often a fatal blow to marriages. As with the other commandments, the tenth commandment overlaps many others. It reeks of idolatry, theft, and a false witness. Left unchecked, it will erode the very foundations of what it means to be married.

Fortunately, the opposite is also true. Marriages that are free from covetousness, both within the marriage and externally, achieve unending trust and intimacy. By remaining focused on what is their own and not lusting after what belongs to another, husbands and wives develop a sense of real security within their marriages. When it comes to overcoming covetousness, the healthy alternative to wanting what is *theirs* is to want what is *yours*. Realizing the greenness of your own grass is the only way to keep from desiring the grass that appears greener on the other side of the fence. It's something that requires concerted effort, and it's a choice. But it's a choice worth making. The ability to value and desire your own circumstances, including your role as your spouse's husband or wife, is transformative. It's the stuff from which satisfaction, love, respect, trust, and happiness grows.

After sealing the covenant between God and the Israelites,

Moses returned to be one with God's bride. God had given Moses two tablets of stone that contained the vows of His marriage to humanity. Carrying the Ten Commandments down from Mount Sinai, Moses surely felt the euphoria of a newlywed bride as she walks down the aisle at end of her wedding. He was glowing.

Upon returning to the Israelites' camp, Moses was assailed by a scene of unbridled covetousness and much more. In his absence, the Israelites had indulged their worst passions. They had lustfully desired to satisfy their own pleasures by forging an idol to replace Yahweh. They made a golden calf. The Israelites created a surrogate for their Husband, so that they could possess Him, own His power, and make Him subservient to their will.

Moses was devastated.

Before he even had the chance to show the *ketubah* to the bride, she had already abandoned her Groom. The revelation came as a shock; the bride had committed adultery during her own wedding. The bride was a whore. She had sold herself to the lowest bidder: herself.

Overwhelmed by the realization that, to the bride, the vows he carried were as dead as the stones they were written on, Moses gave up. He shattered the Ten Commandments. He discarded God's marriage to humanity because humanity had discarded God.

But that was not the end.

Yahweh was not willing to give up that easy.

Even though His bride was not faithful, God was.

Where there is love, there is always hope and forgiveness.

So Yahweh asked Moses to climb the mountain again. This time, Yahweh made Moses carve a set of stone tablets. Perhaps it was a test to see if Moses and His bride were truly willing to try again. Whatever the reason, Moses had to take the first steps. And he did.

Then, God married His Bride. Again.

CHAPTER TEN

The Marriage Commandments

Let nothing come before your spouse.

Do not allow anything or anyone to replace your spouse.

Value the reputation and authority of your spouse.

Remember to set aside time to actively reconnect.

Honor your spouse.

Guard your emotions and reject anger.

Remain faithful and true.

Focus on what you can give and not what you can take.

Be a true witness of your spouse's goodness.

Don't pursue self-centered pleasure.

Made in the USA
Lexington, KY
16 May 2019